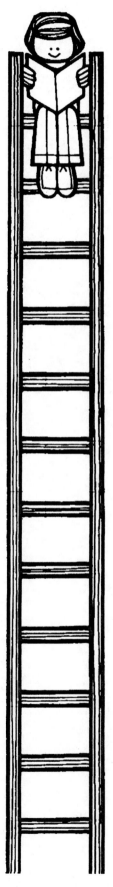

D1370071

The Learning Works

The purchase of this book entitles teachers to reproduce copies of the activities in this book for use in their classroom. The reproduction of any part for an entire school or school system or for commercial use is strictly prohibited.

LW 370

ISBN: 0-88160-301-5

© 1997 Creative Teaching Press, Inc.
Huntington Beach, CA 92649

80544

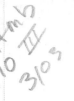

 # Contents

Contents
(continued)

To the Teacher

History Mysteries is designed to acquaint students in grades 4 through 6 with topics in United States history in an engaging and entertaining manner. Each of these two- or three-page activities contains clues to historical facts which students must find with the help of standard reference materials. The facts may be concerned with individuals, events, places, dates, or groups. Several activities require mathematical computation or the sequencing of events.

The content of *History Mysteries* includes all topics common to standard elementary- and middle-school U.S. history curricula, including Native American cultures, European exploration and discovery, colonial America, the Revolution and Civil War, the westward movement, and the lives of Washington and Lincoln. Additional activities on such subjects as the Civil Rights Movement, the immigrant experience, and important or interesting figures in American politics, culture, and folklore will add to students' appreciation of the study of history and will stimulate curiosity and further research. The prospect of solving a mystery or puzzle will provide added motivation. In many activities, the mystery involves finding a lost fortune or document, pursuing a criminal, or identifying incorrect information. In others, the only "mystery" is the information the student is required to find through thought and research.

In most activities, clues are independent of one another, and each one points to a specific fact. Others contain progressive clues, in which students must answer one question before moving on to the next. In the easiest activities, students can find the required facts simply by referencing a name or other obvious entry. In more difficult ones, the clues only hint at starting points for research, and students must apply their higher-level reasoning skills to find the required answer. In a few activities for which students would find it difficult to locate required information without referencing specific names, matching clues are provided. All of the activities in *History Mysteries* can be completed with the aid of standard student reference materials, such as *World Book Encyclopedia* and *Microsoft Encarta*.

To the Teacher
(continued)

Contents

The book is divided into five sections, though the activities need not be presented in any particular order.

Events: Each of these six activities focuses on a broad topic in American history, from the Age of Discovery to the Civil Rights Movement of the mid-20th century.

Famous People: These five activities require students to identify individual figures in such categories as Native American leaders, western pioneers, heroes, and others.

Presidents: These five activities focus on presidents of the United States, with specific attention given to the lives and achievements of George Washington and Abraham Lincoln.

Inventions, Sports, and the Arts: These six activities highlight American achievements in the arts, invention, popular culture, and sports.

Miscellaneous Mysteries: These last five activities call on students to find information on Native American cultures, immigrant groups, monuments and landmarks, legendary figures, and science and technology.

As a whole-class activity: Students can solve a History Mystery as a group, with individuals searching out specific information in texts or reference sources following discussion and brainstorming. Subsequent discussion of an activity can help students place the facts they discover in a wider historical perspective. Completed activity sheets may be placed in students' file folders or portfolios.

As a learning-center activity: Small groups of students may be given an activity to complete cooperatively at a learning center or in the school library. To provide additional motivation, hold time trials of various groups on successful completion of an activity, and devise a point system for order of finish for a class competition.

As an extra-credit or homework activity: Students can be assigned activities to complete using available references at home or in the school or public library. Completed activity sheets may be placed in students' file folders or portfolios.

Events

A Colonial Mystery

"It doesn't seem hard," Linda said. "It says here that to win the new computer, we have to correctly place 10 events on the timeline. They all have to do with the European exploration and colonization of America."

"The rules say you have to place one of these magnets numbered 1 through 10 for each event," said Rafael, reading over her shoulder. "But they don't give you the dates of the events."

"Of course not," Linda replied. "We're going to have to look them up if we can't figure them out from what we already know."

"Then we'd better get started," Rafael said.

1. William Penn founded Pennsylvania as a place of religious freedom. The year he arrived, he made a treaty of peace with the Native Americans of the region. Unlike other English colonists in America, these settlers honored their treaty. Their Indian neighbors respected them in return and never attacked Penn's colony.

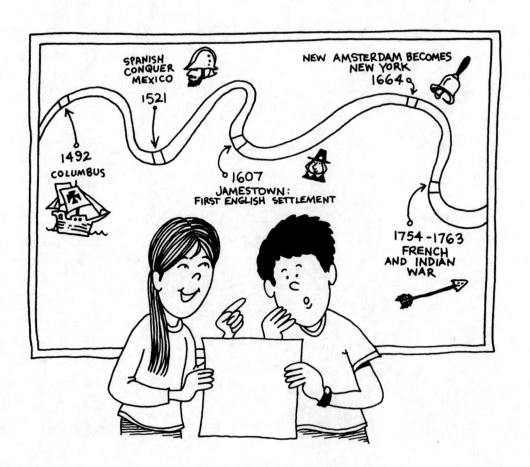

2. Russian explorers led by Vitus Bering and Aleksei Chirikov landed on Kayak Island. This was the first landing by Europeans in what is now Alaska. In the years that followed, Russians built a fur-trading empire that reached as far south as California.

3. Non-free people of African descent in Virginia were made slaves by law. This happened 42 years after the first Africans had been brought to Virginia, not as slaves but as indentured servants. Indentured servants were freed after a fixed number of years, usually seven. The new law said that only white people could be indentured servants. Blacks now became slaves for life.

4. Francisco Vasquez de Coronado set out from Mexico in search of seven fabulous "cities of gold." He never found them, as they did not exist. But Coronado and his men did explore much of the American Southwest, from Arizona to Kansas.

5. Jamestown was the first successful English colony in America. But it was not England's first American colony. The first group of English settlers in the "New World" landed on Roanoke Island, in what is now North Carolina. A second group came two years later. But the colony disappeared mysteriously soon afterward.

6. In early colonial times, most American children did not go to school. The first public schools were set up in Massachusetts. A law in that colony required that each town with at least 50 families use tax money to set up a school for its children.

7. The first successful newspaper in the colonies was published in Boston, beginning in 1704. The most famous colonial newspaper, *The Pennsylvania Gazette,* came along some time later. Most of the paper was written by its printer—Benjamin Franklin.

8. French traders and priests were the first Europeans to explore what would become the American Midwest. Louis Jolliet and Jacques Marquette led an expedition across Wisconsin to the Mississippi River. They were the first non-Indians to explore this area.

9. Wars between European countries often involved their American colonies. The English colonists called one of these conflicts "Queen Anne's War." During this war, Charles Town (later Charleston), South Carolina, was attacked by the French and Spanish.

10. A thousand Puritan settlers led by John Winthrop started the colony of Massachusetts Bay and founded the town of Boston. Over the next 12 years, 16,000 more settlers would join the colony.

Can you help Linda and Rafael place these events in order? Below, write the year in which each event took place. Then write the correct number of each event on the timeline on page 8.

1. _____   6. _____

2. _____   7. _____

3. _____   8. _____

4. _____   9. _____

5. _____   10. _____

The Revolution Turned Upside Down

A chest of gold coins dating from the Revolutionary War is hidden in an attic in a New England farmhouse. G. L. Giles, the heir to the fortune, has stored a map showing the location of the treasure in a computer file. You need a password to open the file. To find it, you need to write the letters of the following events of the war *in the order in which they happened.* When the 10 letters are entered into the computer in the correct order, the map will be yours.

A. The British try to seize weapons stored by patriots in Concord, Massachusetts. Paul Revere and others ride out of Boston to warn the patriot militia. They are waiting for the British near the town of Lexington. Shooting breaks out. The War of Independence has begun.

B. The tiny American army, under George Washington, spends a chilling winter at Valley Forge, Pennsylvania. Nearly a quarter of Washington's soldiers die, but the survivors are molded into a well-trained army.

C. Chased out of New York City by the British, Washington's army retreats northward. The British General Howe misses his chance to destroy them when they escape into New Jersey. New York City, however, will remain in British hands for the rest of the war.

D. Patriotic feeling is aroused when Britain imposes new taxes on its American colonies. The most hated of the taxes requires the colonists to buy stamps to put on newspapers, official documents, even playing cards. Riots break out in several cities over the Stamp Act. Delegates from nine colonies declare that Britain has no right to tax the colonies, as they are not represented in the British Parliament.

History Mysteries
© The Learning Works, Inc.

E. The Battle of Saratoga marks the turning point of the war. A British force under General John Burgoyne is defeated by the Americans, led by General Horatio Gates. Six thousand British troops are taken prisoner. The British plan to cut off New England from the other colonies ends in failure, and France enters the war on the American side.

F. On a stormy Christmas night, Washington leads his army across the Delaware River in an attack on Trenton, New Jersey. A week later, near Princeton, Washington slips past the main British force and defeats a smaller body of British troops who are marching to join them. These two victories greatly raise American spirits.

G. A British army under General Charles Cornwallis defeats an American force under General Gates near Camden, South Carolina. The British are near victory in the South. But Cornwallis cannot decisively beat the Americans, and he wears down his army chasing the American troops across the Carolinas.

H. Massachusetts patriots protest a tax on tea by boarding British ships and throwing the tea into Boston Harbor. The British respond by closing the port of Boston, choking off New England's trade. They send troops to Boston to enforce this and other new laws. The 13 colonies unite in protest against British actions. They choose delegates for a Continental Congress, which meets in Philadelphia.

I. Washington traps Cornwallis's army at Yorktown, Virginia. Cornwallis surrenders his 8,000 troops. As the British lay down their arms, a band plays a tune called "The World Turned Upside Down." Though no peace treaty is signed for another two years, the American victory at Yorktown effectively ends the war.

J. Colonial delegates meeting in Philadelphia declare America's independence from Great Britain. Thomas Jefferson writes the document that announces the birth of a new nation, the United States of America.

Can you figure out the password that will open the computer file? Write the dates with the letters of the clues in the correct order.

1. _____   6. _____

2. _____   7. _____

3. _____   8. _____

4. _____   9. _____

5. _____   10. _____

History Mysteries
© The Learning Works, Inc.

Great-Great-Grandma's Civil War Diary

"I've got a problem here," said the young man on the other side of the desk. He held out a tattered notebook, bound in blue and gray. "This diary was kept by my great-great-grandmother during the Civil War. I inherited it from my aunt. But she didn't take very good care of it. There are places in some entries where the ink has faded. Do you think you could fill in the missing parts?"

"Hmmm," said Rachel Research, historical detective. "It might take some sleuthing in the library, but I think I can help you."

1. *April 16, 1861* Well, they have done it. The fighting has begun. Last week, we took _____ , the Federal fort in Charleston Harbor. Yesterday, Abe Lincoln ordered the Yankee army to take it back. I think once we show those Yankees that we mean to fight for Southern independence, they'll leave us alone.

2. *July 22, 1861* I've never felt prouder to be a rebel! Yesterday our army routed the Yankees near _____ , Virginia, at a stream called Bull Run. It sure is a good thing that Virginia joined our Confederacy. That made it certain that General _____ would be leading our army. His loyalty lies with his home state. They say Lincoln offered him command of the Union army, but he turned it down.

3. *April 18, 1862* News has come from Georgia of a daring raid by northern spies. They were led by a Kentucky gentleman named _____ . They stole a train and set out to burn the bridges along the railroad into Tennessee. That would have cut off supplies to our troops in Virginia. But our boys stopped them, by jiminy!

4. *July 4, 1862* Great news! That Yankee army under General _____ has withdrawn from Richmond! Our General Lee kept him so busy all week he must have thought we had three men to every one of his. Our capital is saved! Another defeat like that, and opinion in the North might turn against Lincoln and the war.

5. *September 25, 1862* Abe Lincoln's gone and freed the slaves. He's issued a document called the _____ . He must have been waiting for a big Northern victory before he did it. I guess that bloody day last week at _____ , in Maryland, counts. After all, it was Lee who retreated after the battle, even though we gave as good as we got.

6. *May 13, 1863* The whole South is in mourning. General _____ is dead. He was the hero of our victory at _____ 12 days ago—as he had been in so many battles. But during the fighting, he was shot accidentally by one of his own men. General Lee said it best: "I have lost my right arm."

7. *July 7, 1863* Bad news on two fronts. Lee's plan to invade the North has failed. The Yankees have pushed him back in a three-day battle at _____ , in Pennsylvania. But even worse is the fall of _____ , Mississippi. Now the Union controls all of the Mississippi River. Could we actually lose this war?

8. *March 11, 1864* The North seems to get stronger every month, while we get weaker. Meanwhile, _____ , that Yankee general who has won all those victories in the West, has been given command of all Northern forces by President Lincoln. He is not a gentleman like our General Lee, but he is a fighter.

9. *Christmas Day, 1864* I cannot believe the stories coming out of Georgia! General _____ 's troops are burning the whole state! They have been stealing everything they can and burning everything they can't steal. Meanwhile, Lee's troops in Virginia are bottled up in the town of _____ . We all speak bravely to one another, but in my heart, I can't believe the South can hold out another year.

10. *April 11, 1865* It is all over. Lee has surrendered his armies to Grant at a place called _____ Court House. At least our boys will be coming home. But the question that is in everyone's minds is—what happens now?

Can you help Rachel fill in the missing names in the diary? Write your answers on the lines below.

1. _____   6. _____

2. _____   _____

   _____   7. _____

3. _____

4. _____   8. _____

5. _____   9. _____

   _____   _____

                              10. _____

Going West

If Mickey "the Mask" Monkfish hadn't been a lover of history, I might never have caught him. He had robbed nine banks, and I was determined that there wouldn't be a tenth. When I looked at the FBI's computer printout, I saw that each of his "jobs" had been near a site that was important in the history of America's expansion westward. The question was, where would he strike next?

1. "The Mask" hit his first bank in a small town near where the states of Virginia, Kentucky, and Tennessee meet. There is a pass here through the Appalachian Mountains. You might say that this is where America's westward movement began. Daniel Boone blazed his "Wilderness Road" through the pass in 1775. Over the next 25 years, more than 200,000 settlers crossed it on their way west.

2. The next robbery took place in a large southern city. First settled by the French, it was the key to the Louisiana Purchase of 1803. President Thomas Jefferson wanted to buy only this port city. Instead, he doubled the size of the United States.

3. Monkfish struck next in a small town in North Dakota. Small town—big city—small town again. Was there a pattern here? There was, but I didn't know it yet. The town turns out to be near a historic fort built by Lewis and Clark. They spent the winter of 1804–1805 here on their expedition to the Pacific Ocean. The fort was named for the Native American tribe who lived there at that time.

History Mysteries
© The Learning Works, Inc.

4. Mickey hit his next bank in a southwestern city that used to be part of Mexico. In 1821, the trader William Becknell opened a trail here from Missouri. Americans came here by wagon to trade. They became aware that Mexico did not have a very strong hold on its northern territories, and that in the event of war, they might be taken over by the United States.

5. The next robbery took place in a city by a lake. It started as a settlement by the Mormons in 1847. They had fled westward from Illinois, seeking religious freedom. "This is the place," said their leader, Brigham Young, when he saw it for the first time. Apparently "the Mask" agreed with him.

6. By now, I was beginning to see Monkfish's pattern. I was not surprised when I saw that his next bank job had taken place in a big city in California. It was here in 1848 that gold was discovered near Sutter's Mill. In less than two years, California's population grew from about 15,000 to more than 100,000.

7. Apparently, "the Mask" was visiting sites in historical order. I was a little surprised to see that he'd pulled his next job near an old fort in Wyoming. After all, the fort had been a busy stopping point on the Oregon Trail *before* the California gold rush. Then I remembered that an important Indian treaty had been signed here in 1851.

8. By now I was on the case, but there was no telling where Mickey would strike next. It turned out to be a city in Kansas. When the railroad reached here in 1867, Texas ranchers began hiring cowboys to drive their cattle to this town. From here they were shipped east by train. The movies have led people to believe that death by gunfire was common in this and other cattle towns. In fact, they were a good deal safer than American cities today!

9. One famous gunfight did take place in an Arizona town in 1881. Wouldn't you know, that's where "the Mask" turned up next. This was the place where Wyatt Earp, his two brothers, and "Doc" Holiday shot it out with a group of ranchers at the O.K. Corral. And here was where Mickey Monkfish robbed the town bank, while actors were reenacting the battle for the tourists.

10. We were reaching the closing of the frontier—and I was closing in on Monkfish. One state had been set aside as "Indian Territory." That ended in 1889, when the territory was opened to white settlement. In the "land rush" of April 22, 50,000 people filed land claims in one day. This future state capital became a city of 10,000 people overnight. I had my agents stationed there. When "the Mask" tried to rob the city's largest bank, it was the end of the trail for him.

Can you identify the cities, towns, forts, and other places the detective was talking about? Write their names on the lines below.

1. _____   6. _____

2. _____   7. _____

3. _____   8. _____

4. _____   9. _____

5. _____   10. _____

Into the 20th Century

Leslie Harriman strode angrily into Roger Keller's antique store. She threw the photo album down on the counter. "You sold me these pictures as 'authentic photographs of bygone America,'" she said. "I now happen to know that every one of them is a fake!"

"How could you possibly think a thing like that?" Roger said smoothly.

"I gave them to my daughter as a present for her tenth birthday," Leslie said. "Ramona knows a great deal about history. She tells me that every page contains one item that could not have existed at the time the photograph is dated. She says someone must have faked them with a computer!"

"Dear me, let's have a look," said Roger.

1. "This photo is dated 1885. It shows a 10-story skyscraper, a horse-drawn streetcar, a man taking a picture of a woman with a small box camera, and, in the background, some boys playing soccer in a schoolyard."

2. "Here we have one dated 1899. A little girl in the photo is laughing at a newspaper comic strip. The headline on the paper reads, 'Americans Debate their New Caribbean Empire.' There's a refrigerator plugged into the wall and a big telephone box next to it."

3. "Here's a crowd going to a baseball game. The caption says, 'Opening game of the World Series, 1901.' People are getting off an electric streetcar. There's a sign on the fence advertising Dunlop tires and an electric light pole on the corner."

4. "Here are some people at an amusement park. There's a Ferris wheel in the background. The little boy in the sailor suit is eating an ice-cream cone. The man in the straw hat is eating a hot dog. Those women are looking into kinetoscopes—old-time movie machines. The caption says, '1895.'"

5. "This family seems to be enjoying an afternoon at home—in 1905. There's a player piano against the wall. The girl is listening to a flat-disk record player—a 'Gramophone.' The man is trying to tune a crystal radio set. The newspaper headline reads, 'Russia, Japan Sign Peace Treaty.'"

6. "This picture is dated 1907. Two women are playing tennis in awkward-looking white dresses. There's an open-top Ford car parked by the tennis court. Electric power lines hang above the street. An advertising sign for cigars reads, 'Don't forget the "Old Man" on Father's Day!'"

7. "Here's one dated 1917. It's nothing but a wall covered with advertising signs. One announces a film of the 1916 Olympic Games. Another announces a public debate: 'Shall We Prohibit Alcohol?' A third advertises a concert—'The Original Dixieland Jazz Band, Direct from New Orleans!' The fourth shows Uncle Sam, saying 'I want YOU for the United States Army!'"

8. "These striking workers are putting down their picket signs to stare up at the sky— apparently at an airplane. There's a billboard that says, 'Eat Your Vitamins,' showing a happy little boy at the supper table. There's a steam-powered fire engine at the curb. The date is given as 1908."

9. "Here are two women in a fashionable restaurant. Their hair is cut short—'bobbed,' I think the style was called. One of them points at a newspaper headline: 'Four Women Jailed for Picketing the White House for Right to Vote.' Another headline refers to a worldwide flu epidemic. A third article reports war news from Europe. The date is 1917."

10. "I love this last one. Here are some people lining up at a movie theater, supposedly in 1920. The movie stars Charles Chaplin. A sign beside the theater advertises 'Cheaper Air Fares to New York.' Another sign reads 'Cox for President—Vote Democratic.' The automobiles by the curb are mostly closed."

"Ah, yes, I see what you mean," Roger Keller said, trying to smile. "This must be someone's idea of a joke. By the way, is your daughter looking for a summer job?"

Could you spot what was wrong with each picture? Identify the faked items on the lines below.

1. _____   6. _____

2. _____   7. _____

3. _____   8. _____

4. _____   9. _____

5. _____   10. _____

A Number of Heroes

The Civil Rights Movement of the 1950s and 1960s secured freedom and respect for many African Americans. Ms. Connors has prepared a quiz on the movement for her class. The only problem is, she isn't a history teacher—she's a math teacher! Her students—and you—need to know both history *and* math to find her "mystery number." Can you do it?

1. Some people say that the Civil Rights Movement started with Jackie Robinson. He was the first African American to be allowed to play major-league baseball since the 1880s. Robinson's fierce courage in the face of racist abuse inspired many blacks. It also got many whites thinking about their attitudes toward race. Begin with the year Robinson first played for the Brooklyn Dodgers.

2. The U.S. Supreme Court ruled in 1954 that separate schools for black and white children violated the U.S. Constitution. This famous law case is known as *Brown v. Board of Education of Topeka.* The lawyer who argued the case later became the first African-American justice named to the Supreme Court. Find the sum of the letters in his first and last names and subtract it from the answer to question 1.

3. On December 1, 1955, Rosa Parks refused to give up her seat on a bus to a white man. She was arrested by the police. Her arrest sparked a boycott of the city's bus system by its black residents. Today this Alabama city is the home of a civil rights museum. Multiply the last answer by the number of letters in its name.

4. The bus boycott was led by a young Baptist minister, Martin Luther King, Jr. His leadership and courage helped hold the boycott together despite pressure from the city's white leaders. His devotion to nonviolent methods and Christian principles won him national respect. Divide the last answer by Dr. King's age at the time the boycott began. (Drop any remainder.)

5. In 1957, trouble broke out in Little Rock, Arkansas. It started over the admission of black students to Central High School. Angry mobs formed. The governor called out the National Guard to prevent the black teenagers from entering the school. Eventually, the United States government stepped in to enforce the desegregation order. Through it all, Daisy Bates, a newspaper editor and community leader, provided help and support to the students. Add to your last answer the number of students who were involved.

6. African-American college students drew national attention in 1960 when they held "sit-ins" at lunch counters and other public places where black people were kept out by "Jim Crow" laws. The sit-in movement spread across the South. That April, students from 56 southern colleges held a meeting. Led by Ella Baker, they formed the Student Nonviolent Coordinating Committee (SNCC). Divide your last answer by the number of letters in the name of the North Carolina city where they met. (Drop any remainder.)

7. Dr. King and other leaders chose Birmingham, Alabama, as a target for an all-out protest against racist laws and customs. In 1962 and 1963, Americans followed the events in Birmingham almost nightly on their TV sets. The nation was particularly shocked by the bombing of a black church on September 15, 1963. Multiply your last answer by the number of children killed by the bomb.

8. The 1964 Mississippi Summer Project was a drive to register blacks to vote. College students who helped on the project were inspired and led by a poor Mississippi woman who had dropped out of school at the age of 13. Her name was Fannie Lou Hamer. Her nationally televised speech that summer gave a stirring voice to the poorest people of the South. She remained active in the movement until she died. Add to your last answer the year of Ms. Hamer's death.

9. Early in 1965, Dr. King, the Reverend Ralph Abernathy, and others led a drive to register blacks to vote. It centered on one Alabama city. The campaign climaxed in a four-day march from this city to the state capital at Montgomery. Divide your last answer by the number of letters in the name of the city.

10. The Voting Rights Act of 1965 brought an end to one phase of the Civil Rights Movement. It gave African Americans political power by allowing the U.S. Government to enforce their right to vote. One result was the election of many African Americans to high office in states where they had previously been barred from voting. In 1989, L. Douglas Wilder was elected governor of one of these states. Subtract from your last answer the number of letters in the name of his state to find the mystery number.

Write the numbers you computed for each clue. Did you find the mystery number?

1. _____   6. _____

2. _____   7. _____

3. _____   8. _____

4. _____   9. _____

5. _____   10. _____

History Mysteries
© The Learning Works, Inc.

Famous People

Vision of a Great Leader

A cold wind was blowing off the plains. It whirled around the mountaintop where I sat staring at the face in the clouds. It was the face of a well-known Native American; of that I was sure. But whose face was it? It kept shifting and shimmering until I was no longer sure whether I was looking at a man or a woman. My heart told me that it would find no peace until I knew who it was.

1. "O face in the clouds," I said, "Are you the Shoshone who guided Lewis and Clark through the Rocky Mountains in 1805? And did that journey reunite you with your people, from whom you had been captured as a child?"

   "No, I am not _____ , nor am I Shoshone," said a voice as gentle as rain. "My people come from further east."

2. "Then are you the chief of the Hunkpapa band of the Sioux? And did you lead your people to victory over General Custer at the Battle of Little Bighorn in 1876?"

   "You are twice wrong," said the voice as loud as thunder. "You are thinking of _____ . I am not he, and he was not a chief. He was a medicine man whose vision guided the Lakota people in their victory that day. I am no warrior on horseback."

Osceola   Susan Picotte   Pontiac

3. "Not on horseback," I mused. "Then are you the legendary Iroquois who united the Five Nations of his people around the year 1400? Did Henry Wadsworth Longfellow write a poem about you?"

   "Twice wrong again." The voice was heavy with sadness. "I am not that leader. And Longfellow's poem was not about him. The poet just used his name. I was indeed a teacher of my people. But I am real, not a legend or a character in a poem."

History Mysteries
© The Learning Works, Inc.

4. "Teacher of your people," I repeated. "Were you a Paiute? Did you set up schools for Native American children in Washington and Nevada? And did you protest the treatment of your people to the President of the United States in 1880?"

"That was not I," the voice cried. "Can't you read a map? I told you I was not from the West."

Ely Parker Hiawatha Sequoyah Sitting Bull

5. "Let me try again," I said. "Are you an Ottawa? Did you try to persuade Indians to stop trading with white people, the better to keep their freedom? And did you unite the tribes of the Midwest in a fight to keep their lands in 1763?"

"No, and nobody named a car after me either!" the voice roared. "Look for me in a later time."

6. "How much later?" I asked, fishing for hints. "Are you the Creek leader who later joined the Seminole after your people were defeated by the Army in 1814? And did you lead the Seminole in a war to keep them from being forcibly removed from their lands?"

"And was I captured by treachery in 1837?" said the voice. "No, I am not he! My leadership took a different form."

Joseph Brant Sacajawea Sarah Winnemucca

7. "Were you the Seneca Iroquois, educated as a lawyer and engineer, who was an officer under General Ulysses S. Grant during the Civil War? And did Grant later name you Commissioner of Indian Affairs when he was president?"

   "Not I," said the voice. "I learned something useful from the 'Americans,' it is true, but it wasn't law or engineering. And I never served in the United States Army."

8. "You were a peacemaker then?" I guessed. "Were you the Omaha woman who became a doctor in 1889 and later set up a hospital? And did you help bring better medical care to rural Nebraska?"

   "A worthy choice, but no," said the voice. "I was a man of peace, but a different sort of teacher."

9. "A religious teacher, perhaps?" I asked, desperate now. "Were you a Mohawk who taught the Christian religion to his people? And did you fight on the British side during the Revolutionary War? Oh, that's right—you said you were a man of peace."

   "*And* a man of letters," said the voice. "But I did side with the British against the American land-grabbers, before I saw the uselessness of war."

10. "Man of letters," I repeated, with sudden insight. "About 86 of them? Did you invent an alphabet of the Cherokee language in 1821?"

    "Well, congratulations," the voice drawled. "It only took you 10 guesses. But at least that puts you 10 steps ahead of most Americans in their knowledge of the First People."

Can you identify the 10 Native Americans suggested by the clues? Write their names on the lines below.

1. _____   6. _____

2. _____   7. _____

3. _____   8. _____

4. _____   9. _____

5. _____   10. _____

O Pioneers!

All the people you will meet on these pages had something to do with exploring or settling the American frontier. No names are given, but somewhere in each clue is a hint that will help you identify the person—if you're resourceful about knowing where to look.

1. "I was born in Haiti. My father may have been French, my mother African. In 1779, I built a trading post on a river the Indians called *Chekagou.* I was the first non-Indian to live permanently along that river. I grew prosperous, and my trading post became the focus of a settlement which later grew into a great city."

2. "I may have done more than anyone to explore and settle the American frontier. I was born in Pennsylvania and died in Missouri, but I am most associated with Kentucky. I first saw the territory in 1769, and I led the first party of settlers there six years later. I explored and hunted well into my eighties, until my eyesight failed."

3. "I was a true-life folk hero of the Wild West. I was born of Mexican parents in the New Mexico territory. As a lawyer and peace officer, I often had to defend Mexican Americans against ill treatment by Anglo settlers. Once I held off a mob of about 80 cowboys for 30 hours while they shot bullets into the hut where I was hiding. After this incident I was known as 'the man who couldn't be killed.' I lived to a ripe old age and died in 1945."

4. "I have a nickname, too. Folks call me 'The Mother of Texas.' I was born in Maryland, but I settled in Texas when it was still Mexican territory. I defended my home and children against attack by Comanche Indians while my husband was away during 1821 and 1822. During that winter I also hunted for our food and gave birth to a baby. I lived in Texas until I died in 1880."

5. "I died in Texas, too, at the Battle of the Alamo in 1836. But I'm best remembered as an inventor. I helped perfect a wickedly effective hunting and fighting knife. Recently, my reputation has suffered from stories that I may have been a pirate and a slave trader. Are the stories true? That's for you to find out!"

6. "Gold was my ruin. I was a Swiss immigrant who built a prosperous trading post in what became the city of Sacramento, California. In 1848, gold was discovered on my land. Gold seekers poured in by the tens of thousands. I lost my land piece by piece, and I died broke."

7. "Some of those gold seekers owed their lives and fortunes to me. I was born in Virginia in 1798, probably in slavery, but I grew up a free man in Missouri. My last name begins with the letter B. I became a fur trader in the Rocky Mountains and lived 12 years with the Crow Indians. In 1850, working as a scout for the United States Army, I discovered a pass through the Sierra Nevada, which served as a route to the gold fields of California. The pass is still named for me."

History Mysteries
© The Learning Works, Inc.

8. "I had a little to do with California, too. They called me 'The Pathfinder.' I was an army officer who explored the Rocky Mountains. During the Mexican War, I helped the North American settlers of California to revolt against Mexican rule. I later settled in California and became a U.S. senator and a candidate for president of the United States."

9. "I was something of a pathfinder myself. In my early twenties, I left Missouri to trap furs in the Rocky Mountains. The fur trade made me rich. Later I operated trading posts on the Great Plains and opened wagon roads through the Rocky Mountains. The routes I blazed later became part of the Oregon Trail, which brought many settlers west. A shortcut on the trail was named for me. Need another hint? If a piglet is a small pig, my name sounds like a small underwater boat."

10. "I was a pioneer settler in colonial Pennsylvania; my last name begins with J and has seven letters. When I was 15, my family was captured by Seneca Indians. When I had the chance to return to my own people, I chose to stay with the Seneca. Both my husbands were American Indian. When I was old, the state of New York gave me some land, but I died on an Indian reservation at the age of 90."

Can you identify these pioneers of American settlement? Write their names on the lines below.

1. _____   6. _____

2. _____   7. _____

3. _____   8. _____

4. _____   9. _____

5. _____   10. _____

Heroes in Peace and War

What makes a person a hero? Bravery in battle? Making a stand for an unpopular cause? Or simply making difficult, courageous choices in one's life? Meet 10 Americans who many people would agree qualify as heroes. Use the clues to find ways to discover their names—and to decide for yourself what heroism can be.

1. This immigrant from Germany was a newspaper printer in colonial New York. In 1734, he printed articles that criticized the British governor of the colony. When he refused to reveal the names of the people who had written the articles, he was thrown in jail and charged with "criminal libel." At his trial he was found not guilty, and his case became the first key victory for American freedom of the press.

2. Our next tale of heroism comes from the Revolutionary War. On the night of April 26, 1777, an exhausted messenger rode up to the door of a colonel of the New York militia. He reported that the British were attacking nearby Danbury, Connecticut, where the local patriots kept a store of weapons. The colonel's troops were at their farms for spring planting and were scattered all over the district. But the colonel had a 16-year-old daughter who was an expert rider. This young hero jumped on her horse and rode 40 miles through the night to round up the men.

3. The most famous conductor on the "Underground Railroad" was this woman, born Araminta Ross. Around 1849, she escaped from slavery in Maryland and fled north to freedom. She later led 19 missions back to the South to bring out other slaves. Altogether, she helped free nearly 300 people, including her husband and parents. She died in 1913 in Auburn, New York.

History Mysteries
© The Learning Works, Inc.

4. Another slave escape was led by this man during the Civil War. He was the pilot of a Confederate steamboat, the *Planter*, which carried messages and weapons between Charleston, South Carolina, and the island forts in Charleston Harbor. On May 13, 1862, with several slave families on board, he piloted the *Planter* past the Confederate guns to the Union ships blockading the harbor. He later became the highest-ranking African American in the Union Navy and served five terms in Congress from South Carolina.

5. The fight for equal rights for women had many heroes, but none greater than this woman. She was a co-founder of the National Woman Suffrage Association in 1869 and fought for the right of American women to vote until her death in 1906. In 1872, she was arrested and fined for voting in Rochester, New York.

6. This Nez Percé chief lived in Oregon's Wallowa Valley. In 1877, fighting broke out when the government tried to remove his people and settle them on a reservation in Idaho. The chief led a masterful 1,000-mile retreat across parts of three states. When he was forced to surrender, he declared "I will fight no more forever." His retreat is still studied by young officers in military colleges.

7. The first woman to be elected to the U.S. Congress served the state of Montana. During her first weeks in office in 1917, she voted against U.S. entry into World War I. For this unpopular stand, she was voted out of office the next year. In 1940, she was elected to Congress again—and cast the only vote against American entry into World War II.

8. This soldier of World War I had sought to stay out of the army for religious reasons. But as a farm boy growing up in Tennessee, he had become an expert shot with rifle and pistol. On October 8, 1918, he was a member of a patrol that was ordered to take out a German machine-gun "nest." He killed 20 enemy soldiers and forced a German officer to surrender 132 prisoners. Later he was awarded the Congressional Medal of Honor.

9. In 1941, African Americans in the U.S. Navy were allowed to serve only as stewards, cooks, or waiters. On December 7, this steward was serving on board the battleship *West Virginia* at Pearl Harbor, Hawaii, when it came under Japanese attack. Though he had no training as a gunner, he took over the machine gun of a seaman who had been killed and shot down four enemy planes. His last name has six letters, beginning with M.

10. This Arizona-born farm boy of Mexican descent saw his family lose their land during the Great Depression and become migrant laborers. Later, he organized the first successful farm-workers union. He won recognition for the United Farm Workers during a long and successful strike against California grape growers from 1965–1970 and continued to lead the UFW until his death in 1993.

Did you identify these 10 heroes by their deeds? Write their names on the lines below.

1. _____	6. _____
2. _____	7. _____
3. _____	8. _____
4. _____	9. _____
5. _____	10. _____

In a Man's World

Few people today think twice about a woman being a doctor, astronaut, business leader, or United States senator. But not so long ago, a woman faced barriers of resistance, prejudice, and disapproval if she tried to make her way in the public world that men claimed as their own. Can you identify the American women pictured here, each a barrier-breaker in her own way?

1. I was the first American woman to graduate from medical school, after 29 other medical schools had turned me down. When I set up my practice in New York City, I was barred from working in hospitals. In 1857, I opened my own hospital in partnership with my sister, also a doctor, where we specialized in treating poor women and children. Later, we started a medical school for women.

2. When I was 16 years old, I was running my father's plantation in South Carolina while he was away in the West Indies. When my husband died, after 14 years of marriage, I managed his lands for 35 years. By sharing my farming techniques with other South Carolina planters, I helped build the economy of the colony and was honored by George Washington. Two of my sons became prominent politicians. One was a signer of the Constitution of the United States.

3. I, too, was from South Carolina, but my sister Angelina and I moved to Philadelphia in the 1820s because of our opposition to slavery. We were both active in the antislavery movement and in the women's rights movement, writing essays on behalf of both causes. Because we argued that the struggle for women's equality was equally as important as the abolition of slavery, we faced bitter opposition from some of the men in the movement.

Nellie Tayloe Ross

Sarah Grimké

Mary Lease

4. My real name was Elizabeth Cochrane, but I was better known by a pen name. As a reporter for a New York newspaper, I posed as a thief in order to write about how women prisoners were treated by the police, and as a woman who was mentally ill to report on conditions in mental hospitals. But I am best remembered for my trip around the world in 1889–1890. I made the journey in 72 days, beating the "record" of Phileas Fogg, the fictional hero of Jules Verne's novel, *Around the World in 80 Days.*

Elizabeth Blackwell

Eleanor Roosevelt

Nellie Bly

Lillian Wald

5. I was born in Pennsylvania but moved to Kansas as a young woman. I became a leader of the Farmers' Alliance Movement, which fought the exploitation of American farmers by railroads and banks. In my speeches, I urged Kansas farmers to "raise less corn and more *hell.*" In the 1890s, I helped found the Populist Party, which elected many candidates to Congress from the Midwest, West, and South.

6. While working as a nurse's aide in World War I, I became interested in aviation. I earned a pilot's license and began flying in air shows. I became the first woman to fly across the Atlantic Ocean, and later the first woman to fly the Atlantic solo. In 1937, I disappeared mysteriously while on an around-the-world flight.

7. I was born a slave in Mississippi. As a young woman in Memphis, Tennessee, I became part owner of a newspaper, *Free Speech.* It was after three of my friends were lynched that I began to crusade against the violence and murder directed against African Americans. I later continued my work in Chicago, struggling without success to persuade Congress to pass an anti-lynching law.

History Mysteries
© The Learning Works, Inc.

8. I was born into a wealthy family New York City. As a nurse, I began to investigate the health problems of poor immigrants, especially immigrant children. In 1893, I established a settlement house devoted to nursing care for the poor. Later I advised Presidents William Howard Taft and Woodrow Wilson on children's health and other issues.

9. I was the niece of one president of the United States and became the wife of another. "First Ladies" before me had confined their duties to hosting White House parties. I became an active member of my husband's administration, making "fact-finding" trips throughout the United States and other countries and advising him on national policy. Later I became a delegate to the United Nations and a leader in the Democratic Party.

10. If my "barriers" weren't as strong as those my sisters had to face, it was because I lived in "the equality state." It was my state that first gave women the right to vote and let us serve on juries. And in 1925, it became the first state to have a woman governor—me.

Can you identify these 10 women? Write their names on the lines below.

1. _____   6. _____

2. _____   7. _____

3. _____   8. _____

4. _____   9. _____

5. _____   10. _____

Amelia Earhart

Elizabeth Pinckney

Ida Bell Wells

American Originals and Great Spirits

"There are some people in our history," said Mr. Eagle, "who seem to represent the American spirit more than others. You read about their lives, and it seems as though they could not have lived anywhere else. They were not all great people, or even good people. But they all seem in some way or another to stand for what we Americans like to think we are."

"Like whom?" asked several students in the class.

"See if you can name some of them," Mr. Eagle said.

1. "Everyone knows our first American original. He was a writer and publisher, an inventor, an experimenter with electricity, a statesman, and an ambassador. He started the first American postal system and the first public library and public hospital. When he signed the Declaration of Independence in his home city, he was 70 years old and the most respected man in the new United States."

2. "Now let's meet a woman, a slave set free when the state of New York abolished slavery in 1828. She was born Isabella Baumfree, but she took another name after an experience in which she believed that God had commanded her to preach. She became one of the greatest abolitionist speakers, traveling throughout the northern states to preach against slavery, but she gave her most famous speech at a women's rights convention in Ohio in 1851."

3. "If you're ever near Concord, Massachusetts, stop by Walden Pond. One American original spent two years there, trying to live alone with nature. He wrote a book, *Walden,* based on his experience. He is also known for his essay, 'Civil Disobedience.' In it he stated that individual conscience is a higher authority than the government, and that people should refuse to obey a law they feel is unjust. He was tested in this belief in 1846 when he was jailed for refusing to pay taxes in protest against slavery and the Mexican War."

History Mysteries
© The Learning Works, Inc.

4. "One of our greatest poets celebrated the American spirit in his book, *Leaves of Grass.* He first published it himself in 1855—it was so unusual that no book publisher would have anything to do with it. His poems express his love of the United States and his belief in its special qualities, but they also celebrate life and the unity of all humankind. His most popular poem, 'O Captain! My Captain!' is about the death of Abraham Lincoln.

5. "Let's now turn to a showman, a producer of concerts and circus acts. He promoted his shows with outrageous advertising and outright lies. He opened his famous circus in 1871 and later called it 'The Greatest Show on Earth.' He died in 1891, but people today still enjoy the circus he founded. Though he probably never really said, 'There's a sucker born every minute,' few would consider him a great spirit. But an American original? Certainly!"

6. "Do you enjoy hiking, camping, or visiting national parks? If so, you have this next man to thank. Born in Scotland in 1838, he grew up on a farm in Wisconsin. He became a farmer, inventor, and scientist, but what he loved best was exploring wilderness areas. His influence led the government to set aside hundreds of millions of acres of land for national parks and forests."

7. "One American original lived most of her life in France, though she was born in Pennsylvania in 1874. As a young writer experimenting with new styles, she settled in Paris in 1903. Her own words are little remembered today, except for one line of poetry—'Rose is a rose is a rose.' But her style greatly influenced other writers, and her home was a meeting place for artists who created the look of the twentieth century."

8. "Now consider this woman, born in Alabama in 1880. By age two, after an illness, she was blind, deaf, and mute. But with the help of a teacher, Anne Sullivan, she learned to write, to read in Braille, and to speak. She went on to college and spent the rest of her life working to improve the lives of people who were blind and deaf."

9. "Now, how about a baseball player, one of the greatest pitchers of all time? He didn't appear in the major leagues until 1948, because of the unwritten rule that kept black players out. But he was a star in the Negro leagues as early as 1924, when he may have been just 18 years old—no one knows for sure. He was famous for his down-home humor, particularly this guideline for staying young: 'Don't look back—something might be gaining on you!'"

10. "Finally, we honor a singer and composer of folk songs, born in Oklahoma in 1912. He spent much of his life traveling the United States, beginning when he was about 16 years old. Many of his songs describe the lives of ordinary Americans and people made poor by the Great Depression. But he also wrote many songs celebrating America, including 'This Land is Your Land.'"

Can you identify these American originals and great spirits? Write their names on the lines below.

1. _____   6. _____

2. _____   7. _____

3. _____   8. _____

4. _____   9. _____

5. _____   10. _____

History Mysteries
© The Learning Works, Inc.

Presidents

George Washington's Lost Diary

I'd found it in a desk in an old Virginia farmhouse. It was a plain old notebook, bound in faded blue. It *seemed* to be George Washington's long-lost diary. Some of the entries were so worn, I couldn't read the words and names he had written. It was only after doing a little research that I was able to make some sense of the book—and prove beyond a doubt that it was a fake!

1. *March 25, 1748* I am camped here in the wilderness of northern Virginia. _____ has hired me to survey his considerable land holdings. It was quite a job to give to a 16-year-old boy, even if he is a cousin of my brother's wife. But I like being a land surveyor, and this trip is making a man of me.

2. *October 28, 1753* Great news! _____ , the acting governor, has approved me for bearing his message to the French commander at Fort Le Boeuf. The governor means to warn the French to keep their troops out of the Ohio River Valley. If they refuse, it will mean war. I have been a soldier only eight months, and I am honored to be trusted with the mission.

3. *May 28, 1754* Moving on _____ , the French command post at the forks of the Ohio, I captured a group of prisoners today, with the loss of only one of my men. It seems I am well suited to soldiering. I am still angry, however, that as a colonial militiaman I am paid less than an officer of my rank in the regular British army. All the Americans resent this policy, which is plainly unfair.

History Mysteries
© The Learning Works, Inc.

4. *June 4, 1765* Quite a stir here in Williamsburg over the Stamp Act! The words "No taxation without representation!" seem to be on everyone's lips. In all my years in the House of Burgesses, I have never heard such angry speeches. Young _____ of Hanover County is quite a firebrand. He's the lawyer who won the Parson's Cause suit two years ago. He was just elected to the House, and he is already one of its most powerful speakers.

5. *June 15, 1775* Congress has named me commander-in-chief of our forces. I did not seek the position. Most of us believed that it would go to John Hancock of Massachusetts. But _____ , a Massachusetts man himself, proposed my name. He said my popularity would help unite the colonies. Now that I have been chosen, I will do everything I can to carry out my command.

6. *February 24, 1780* We are still encamped at _____ , awaiting the spring thaw. This winter has been as harsh as the one two years ago at Valley Forge. The men are starving, though it was a bountiful year across the country. Lack of supplies has proven a more formidable enemy to us than the British army.

7. *May 25, 1787* The delegates here in Philadelphia have elected me their president. I truly hope we can agree on some effective reforms to the Articles of Confederation. Without a federal government, we are a weak nation, hardly a nation at all. This was proven last year by that man, _____ , in Massachusetts. That mob he led threatened the rights of property. The militia stopped them, but only after months of near-anarchy.

8. *September 17, 1787* Let us hope this new Constitution of ours will make us a lasting nation. If it does, posterity will have _____ to thank. He is a Virginian, a close friend of Jefferson's, and it was he who kept careful notes on the debates and negotiated the compromises among our squabbling states.

9. *April 30, 1789* With the greatest reluctance, today I took office as the first president of the United States. I truly wished to live out my life at Mount Vernon, but I have been called upon yet again to serve my country. Congress has kindly provided us with a fine house here in _____ , which will be the nation's capital until they complete the new Federal city on the Potomac that they are naming for me.

10. *May 1, 1796* I will be grateful to leave public office next year. The partisan quarrels between Jefferson and _____ , my Secretary of the Treasury, have left me with a profound distaste for politics. The president should be above the personal attacks that I have had to suffer. I shall be the most grateful man in America when I can at last retire to my farm.

Can you identify the 10 people and places whose names were left blank? And can you spot the clue that proves the diary a fake? Write them on the lines below.

1. _____   6. _____

2. _____   7. _____

3. _____   8. _____

4. _____   9. _____

5. _____   10. _____

_____

_____

•45•

Searching for Abraham Lincoln

The e-mail message appeared mysteriously on my computer. It told me I'd find a suitcase full of money at a key place in the life of Abraham Lincoln. I was curious. A suitcase full of money sounded too good to be true—but I love a good mystery.

1. I started out in the county where Lincoln was born, on February 12, 1809. As everyone knows, he was born in a log cabin on a farm near Hodgenville. That did not mean his family was poor, however. They had a good farm, and there was always food on the table. But there were no suitcases full of money lying around.

2. I went next to a rural county in Indiana. When Abraham was seven, his family bought a farm here. One reason they moved was that his father, Tom Lincoln, did not like slavery, and Indiana was a free state. Abe grew up chopping trees, splitting rails, reading by candlelight, and amusing his neighbors by telling stories in the village store. I visited all the Lincoln sites in the county, but found no money.

3. I found none at my next stop, either. As a matter of fact, I spent most of what I brought with me. When Lincoln was 22, a trader hired him and two other young men to take a flatboat to this city. It gave young Abe his first close look at Southern slavery. According to a legend, he told one of his companions, "If I ever get the chance to hit slavery, I'll hit it hard."

4. Lincoln lived most of his life in Illinois, starting with the town I tried to visit next. He clerked in a store, and later was a partner in a store of his own. Here he won election to the state legislature and studied law. Lincoln left the town because it was losing population. Today, I discovered, it's not even there any more.

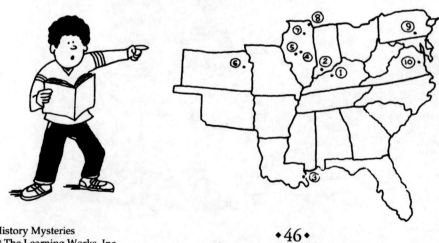

5. In 1837, Lincoln moved to the new state capital. Here he practiced law for 23 years, married, and raised his children. He served one term in Congress and made good money as a lawyer—but he didn't leave any in a suitcase for me.

6. Lincoln was never in the Kansas town I visited next, but I had a hunch. In 1856, the town was the scene of bloody violence over whether slavery should be extended into free territories. The controversy made Lincoln a leading spokesman against the extension of slavery. It brought him into opposition with Stephen A. Douglas, another Illinois politician. It's a nice town, the home of the University of Kansas. But whenever I asked about Abe Lincoln and a suitcase full of money, people gave me funny looks.

7. In 1858, Lincoln ran against Douglas for the U.S. Senate. Their public debates attracted national attention. I went to the town where the first debate was held, on August 21, 1858. Anywhere that Lincoln went, there seems to be a monument of some sort. But I was beginning to feel like a monumental fool.

8. Next I went to the city where Lincoln received the Republican Party's nomination for president in 1860. It's been the site of many nominating conventions since then. But I didn't even bother to look for the money there. I wouldn't have known where to start.

9. Of course when he was president, Lincoln lived in Washington, D.C. Northwest of there is a town where the greatest battle of the Civil War was fought. It was also where Lincoln gave his most famous speech. I made a donation to the battlefield memorial.

10. Oh, I found the money, all right. It was in the White House—the *Confederate* White House, in the city that was the Southern capital during the Civil War. Lincoln came here after its capture by the Union Army. The suitcase had been left with my name on it. It was indeed full of money—*Confederate* money. I never did find out who played that joke on me. But I suppose Abe Lincoln, who loved a good joke as well as anyone, would have appreciated it.

Can you name these counties, towns, and cities associated with Abraham Lincoln? Write their names, together with the names of their states, on the lines below.

1. _____   6. _____

2. _____   7. _____

3. _____   8. _____

4. _____   9. _____

5. _____   10. _____

He Said *What?*

"It's a simple task," the boss said. "We're developing a new CD-ROM tour of the White House. Here and there, video images of the presidents pop up and give quotes from their speeches and writings."

"Cool," I said. "But how does anyone know what Jefferson and Lincoln and those guys sounded like?"

"Never mind that," the boss said. "The programmer knows a lot about voice synthesis, but nothing about history. We have *here* a tape of sound bites . . . and *here* some very clever videos of past presidents. Your job is to put them together so that each president speaks the correct words."

"Ask not what your company can do for you," I said, staring at the tapes, "ask what you can do for your company."

1. "And so, my fellow Americans, ask not what your country can do for you; ask what you can do for your country."

2. "Speak softly and carry a big stick; you will go far."

3. "A government of laws, and not of men."

4. "If you can't stand the heat, get out of the kitchen."

5. "The chief business of the American people is business."

History Mysteries
© The Learning Works, Inc.

6. "What country before ever existed a century and a half without rebellion? . . . . The tree of liberty must be refreshed from time to time with the blood of patriots and tyrants. It is its natural manure."

7. "All of our people, all over the country—except the pure-blooded Indians—are immigrants or descendants of immigrants . . . ."

8. "As I would not be a *slave*, so I would not be a *master*. This expresses my idea of democracy. Whatever differs from this, to the extent of the difference, is no democracy."

9. "There are no necessary evils in government. Its evils exist only in its abuses. If it would confine itself to equal protection, and . . . shower its favors alike on the rich and the poor, it would be an unqualified blessing."

10. "People have got to know whether or not their president is a crook. Well, I'm not a crook."

Can you match the presidents with their quotes? Write their names on the lines below.

1. _____   6. _____

2. _____   7. _____

3. _____   8. _____

4. _____   9. _____

5. _____   10. _____

Monuments to the Unknown

George Washington. Thomas Jefferson. Abraham Lincoln. These are presidents whose names almost everyone knows. Other presidents are not so well remembered. Yet they, too, served in our nation's highest office, and important events happened during their terms. In fact, some of the events are better known than the presidents! Suppose you were to find 10 monuments, each commemorating four events. Could you identify the president whose name might be carved on each monument, and name the dates of his presidency?

1. Railroads first linked New York and Chicago.
   American ships opened up trade with Japan.
   Harriet Beecher Stowe's novel *Uncle Tom's Cabin* turned many northern Americans against southern slavery.
   Isaac Singer invented the first continuous-stitch sewing machine.

2. Noah Webster published his first *Webster's Dictionary*.
   Garment workers in New York City formed the first American women's labor union.
   Jedediah Smith led an expedition overland to California.
   The Erie Canal was completed, connecting the Atlantic Ocean with the Great Lakes.

History Mysteries
© The Learning Works, Inc.

3. The first baseball game with rules resembling those of today was played at Hoboken, New Jersey.

   A national convention in support of women's rights was held at Seneca Falls, New York.

   A famine in Ireland sent a great wave of immigrants to the United States.

   War with Mexico added new territory to the United States.

4. The first movie studio was built in Hollywood, California.

   The "unsinkable" ship *Titanic* sank on its first voyage.

   American explorers Robert Peary and Matthew Henson led the first successful expedition to the North Pole.

   Airplanes were first used in warfare.

5. The Empire State Building was completed in New York City.

   Iowa artist Grant Wood painted "American Gothic."

   A stock market crash led to the Great Depression.

   The planet Pluto was discovered by astronomer Clyde Tombaugh.

6. Former high government officials were given jail sentences in the Watergate scandal.

   Alex Haley's book *Roots,* describing his search for his African ancestors, was a best-seller.

   Women were admitted to the United States Military, Naval, and Air Force academies for the first time.

   The Vietnam War, America's longest armed conflict, ended.

7. Herman Hollerith invented the punched-card tabulating machine, an early ancestor of the computer.
   Ellis Island opened as a United States immigration station.
   The Johnstown Flood ravaged Pennsylvania.
   Yosemite National Park opened.

8. Mount St. Helens, a volcano, erupted in Washington state.
   Americans were held hostage in Iran for 444 days.
   The first "test tube baby" was born.
   The movie *Star Wars* broke box-office records.

9. Robert H. Goddard developed and tested the first rocket.
   John Scopes was put on trial in Dayton, Tennessee, for teaching the theory of evolution to high-school students.
   Nellie Tayloe Ross was the first woman to become governor of an American state (Wyoming).
   Charles Lindbergh made the first solo airplane flight across the Atlantic Ocean.

10. The first public telephones were installed in Boston.
    The game of Bingo was invented.
    Thomas Edison invented sound recording and electric lights.
    Federal troops left the South, ending the Reconstruction Period after the Civil War.

Could you identify all of the presidents? How many did you get on the first clue? The second? Write their names and the years of their presidencies below.

1. _____   6. _____

2. _____   7. _____

3. _____   8. _____

4. _____   9. _____

5. _____   10. _____

Presidents by the Numbers

A letter written by Thomas Jefferson is hidden in a locker at the railroad station in Washington, D.C. This rare and valuable document is yours if you can find the number of the locker. Answer these questions about the presidents, and you can discover the number—*if* you do the math correctly!

1. The largest man ever to be president tipped the scales at 327 pounds. After he was president, he served as chief justice of the United States. Start with the year he was voted out of office.

2. This president was a commanding general in the Mexican War. He had little chance to prove himself as president; he died after only 16 months in office. One of his daughters was married to another president—Jefferson Davis, President of the Confederacy during the Civil War. Find the number that represents the last two digits of the year our mystery man died and subtract it from your last answer.

3. The first president to travel to Europe while in office went to Paris, France, in 1919 to help negotiate the peace conference following the end of World War I. He proposed a famous series of "points" to be used as guidelines for preserving world peace. Divide your last answer by the number of points in his program.

4. This president fought in the Revolutionary War and was wounded at the Battle of Trenton. Later, he was a neighbor of Thomas Jefferson, and became his political ally. He served as secretary of state during a war that is usually identified by the year it started. Add that year to your last answer.

5. Only one man has ever been elected to two nonconsecutive terms as president. He also was the first president ever to get married while occupying the White House. Divide your last answer by the last digit of the year he took the oath of office for his first term.

6. A career army officer, this president was the commanding general of Allied forces in World War II. He planned the invasion of Normandy, in northern France, that led to the defeat of Nazi Germany. Subtract from your last answer the last two digits of the year of this invasion.

7. This president, too, had been a victorious commanding general. But as president, he surrounded himself with corrupt officials, and his presidency was marked by scandal. A national depression set off by bank failures also damaged his reputation. Divide the last answer by the last digit of the year this depression began.

8. Scandals also brought down another president, whose death in 1923 has long been rumored to have been a suicide. He had appointed too many personal friends to high government office. Long before their dishonesty was fully known, they were often called "the _____ gang," after their home state. Multiply your last answer by the number of letters in the name of that state.

9. This president was known as a warrior. He resigned his post as Assistant Secretary of the Navy in 1898 and raised a cavalry regiment to fight in the Spanish-American War. Despite this, he became the first president to win the Nobel Peace Prize, for negotiating the settlement of a war between Russia and Japan. Add to your last answer the last two digits of the year in which he was awarded the Nobel Peace Prize.

10. This president signed landmark civil rights laws and sought to end poverty in America. He was driven from office, however, by nationwide protests against his decision to increase American involvement in the Vietnam War. To find the number of the locker, subtract from your last answer the last two digits of the year he announced he would not seek another term as president.

Write the name of each president and the numbers you computed for each clue. Did you find the number of the locker?

1. _____   6. _____

2. _____   7. _____

3. _____   8. _____

4. _____   9. _____

5. _____   10. _____

Inventions, Sports, and the Arts

Literary Treasure Hunt

A rich, eccentric librarian has left $100,000 in cash in a safe-deposit box. A key and pieces of a message revealing the location of the box are hidden in 10 books at the public library. But which books? The librarian has left clues to the identity of their authors. Can you match the clues to the books pictured here?

1. The author spent several years working on boats and later wrote a book about his or her experiences. The author did *not* work on an ocean-going ship or write novels about sea voyages.

2. The author read one of his or her poems at the inauguration of a president of the United States. The author did *not* write about New England.

3. The author is equally famous for poetry and prose. The author did *not* write a famous biography of Abraham Lincoln.

4. The author wrote several children's books about the same family. The author did *not* serve as a nurse during the Civil War.

5. The author lived and wrote for many years hidden away in a room of his or her parents' home. The author did *not* write novels.

6. The author wrote poetry for adults, and also several books of humorous stories for children. The author did *not* write his or her children's stories in verse.

7. The author was born in New York City. The author's greatest and most famous book was *not* considered a success during his or her own lifetime.

8. The author wrote most of his or her books under a pen name. The author was *not* born in Missouri.

9. The author was born in San Francisco, California, and wrote poetry. The author did *not* write about California.

10. The author's father was friends with several of the most famous American writers of his day. The author's books for adults were *not* as successful as his or her books for children.

Can you identify the authors from the clues? Write their names on the lines below.

1. _____   6. _____

2. _____   7. _____

3. _____   8. _____

4. _____   9. _____

5. _____   10. _____

History Mysteries
© The Learning Works, Inc.

The Great Music and Dance Forum

A mysterious tape has arrived in your mailbox. It seems to be a recorded conversation among 10 great American musicians and dancers. It can't be genuine—after all, most of these people are dead! But just suppose these artists had somehow been able to sit down together and talk about themselves. You might not recognize their voices, but would you know them by their accomplishments?

1. "I suppose it's right that I should begin. I was America's first composer of note—pardon the pun. I dedicated my *Seven Songs for the Harpsichord* to George Washington. I was also a lawyer, an artist, and, as a New Jersey delegate to the Continental Congress, a signer of the Declaration of Independence."

2. "Yes, you set a pattern for American classical musicians that lasted well into my day. I wrote symphonies, piano music, and songs. But my music was rather unusual, and I couldn't make a living at it. Luckily, I ran a successful insurance business. My music reflects my upbringing in Danbury, Connecticut. It's full of references to holidays, places in New England, patriotic songs, even baseball. My *Third Symphony* won the 1947 Pulitzer Prize, but by then I was over 70 years old."

3. "I don't believe I ever danced to your music, though I might have. I was born in San Francisco in 1877, and my dances were as experimental as your compositions. I studied ballet, but I became bored with its old-fashioned formalism. I created a modern form of dance, inspired by poetry, art, and nature. Later I set up schools of dance for children in several countries."

4. "I started writing songs for the theater as a teenager in New York City. I loved jazz, which was becoming popular when I was young, but I also studied classical music. My most famous pieces, *Rhapsody in Blue* and the opera *Porgy and Bess,* combine both types of music. I also wrote dozens of popular songs which are still heard today, more than 60 years after my death."

5. "I would say that jazz *is* the classical music of America—and no one did more than I to make it so, if I do say so myself. I organized a jazz orchestra to play my music. Beginning in 1927, we played dance music at the Cotton Club in the Harlem district of New York City. Later, after we became world famous, I wrote longer compositions based on African-American history and religious themes. I died in 1974, but my orchestra is still going strong."

6. "I was one of the first American natives to become a world-class ballerina—and also the first Native American. I was born to the Osage tribe in Oklahoma in 1925. I created many dances during my 18 years with the New York City Ballet, and later I started my own ballet company in Chicago."

7. "I, too, organized my own dance company, in 1958, when I was 27 years old. Seven years later, I quit dancing and devoted myself full time to choreography. I composed dances for my own company and others. Many of my dances, including my most famous work, *Revelations,* were inspired by my African-American and Southern heritage."

History Mysteries
© The Learning Works, Inc.

8. "I was one of the first American-born musicians to direct a major symphony orchestra—the New York Philharmonic, beginning in 1958. By then, I was already well known as a composer, both of symphonic works and of music for the theater. I appeared often on TV, playing and discussing classical music and introducing it to a wide audience. I'm probably best known for my 1957 musical, *West Side Story*, which was made into a popular movie."

9. "As you may know, I often worked with the last speaker. Born in New York City in 1918, I became a solo dancer with American Ballet Theater when I was 24 years old. Two years later, I made my debut as a choreographer with my ballet *Fancy Free*, and I have created many dances since then. But I am probably best known as a director of musical plays on Broadway."

10. "I'm on Broadway, too, as director of the 'Jazz at Lincoln Center' program in New York City. I was born in New Orleans in 1961. My father and brothers are jazz musicians. I was trained from the age of 12 to be a jazz trumpet player, but I soon became interested in classical music as well. By age 22, I had won awards for my recordings of both types of music."

Can you name these giants of American music and dance? Write their names on the lines below.

1. _____   6. _____

2. _____   7. _____

3. _____   8. _____

4. _____   9. _____

5. _____   10. _____

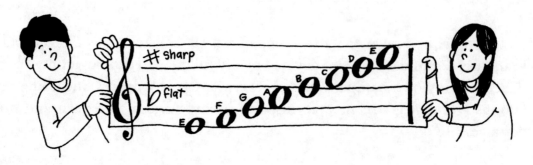

Painting of Mystery

"I have behind this curtain a work of art by a great American artist," the dealer said with a wicked smile. "This valuable piece is yours, *if* you can guess the identity of the artist."

"Sounds easy," I said confidently. "Let's see it."

"Oh, no, you don't get to *see* it," said the dealer, standing protectively in front of the curtain. "But I will let you ask 10 questions about it, and give you clues. Do you still think it's easy?"

"I guess I'm going to find out," I said.

1. "Is the painting a seascape?" I asked.

    "No, nothing to do with the sea at all," the dealer said. "The artist did not live in Maine and was not particularly interested in sailors or fisherman. One down."

2. "Very well, forget the sea," I said. "Is the painting a landscape—a desert scene, perhaps? A cow's skull in the sand, maybe, or a Native American pueblo?"

    "No, nothing to do with New Mexico," the dealer cackled. "And the artist was not born in Wisconsin, and was never married to a famous photographer. No, it's not a landscape, or a seascape, or any kind of scape at all."

3. I was beginning to feel like a scape*goat*. "Let's try people, then," I said. "Does the picture show a mother and child?"

    "You're thinking of that Pennsylvania artist who settled in France in 1866—the Impressionist painter," said the dealer. "No, not that one. This artist is as American as the prairie—never lived in Europe."

4. "The prairie," I repeated. "Did the artist live in Missouri, and paint scenes of frontier life—fur traders on the river, and small-town elections?"

    "And cows in their stalls, and rifle-shooting contests?" the dealer mocked. "Sorry—wrong again."

5. "Let's go farther west," I said grimly. "Did the artist travel to Montana from New York at the age of 20? Are we talking about action paintings of Indians and cowboys, and sculpture, too?"

"This is boring," sighed the dealer. "No, it wasn't that painter whose name sounds like a rifle. Try again."

6. *No* painting is worth this, I thought, no matter how valuable it may be. Wait a minute—he never said it was a painting. He said 'work of art.' Maybe it was a sculpture! Or even—

"Let me ask you this," I said. "When you said 'prairie,' did you mean the 'prairie style' of architecture? Is it perhaps a design of a house by a great American architect?"

"Oh, that Chicago person whose buildings blend so nicely with their natural surroundings? No; didn't I say it was a painting?"

7. "Let's go back to the early days," I said. "Was this artist famous in colonial times? Was it someone who painted historical scenes, and taught many American artists of the early 1800s?"

"I told you, the artist didn't live in Europe," said the dealer impatiently. "The one you're thinking of settled in London in the 1760s. Next question, please."

8. "This is getting *very* old," I said tiredly. "Wait a minute—*old!* Was this artist known by a nickname that suggests old age? Is it someone who didn't begin painting until the age of 76, and was still going strong at 100?"

"No, this artist died at 85 and did not paint pretty scenes of country life," the dealer said.

9. "Maybe I should forget 'scenes,'" I said. "Is it the Wyoming-born artist who did those 'drip' paintings in the 1940s and '50s? The one who practically invented abstract expressionism?"

"I can't stand abstract art," the dealer sighed. "Wouldn't touch it. I like a picture that looks like a picture."

10. "I have one question left," I said. "Is it a painter from New York who painted realistic scenes—almost like photographs? Someone who died in 1967 and whose most famous painting is of lonely people in an all-night diner? Is it _____ ?"

As I carried the painting out of the gallery, the dealer was screaming and stamping his foot. You'd almost have thought that the artist's name was Rumpelstiltskin!

Can you identify the 10 artists suggested by the clues? Write their names on the lines below.

1. _____   6. _____

2. _____   7. _____

3. _____   8. _____

4. _____   9. _____

5. _____   10. _____

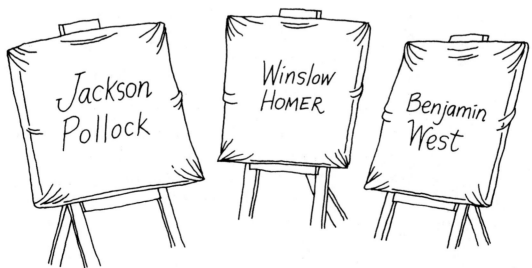

Pop! Goes America

Welcome to the museum of American popular culture. The United States has not always had video games, rock and roll music, or television. But Americans have always had ways to entertain themselves, popular fads, and celebrities. Step into our exhibit hall, and see if you can identify the people associated with these artifacts and curiosities of American pop.

1. Take this old magazine, for instance—"Godey's Lady's Book." Look at the pictures, and you'll see how middle-class Americans lived 150 years ago. Founded in 1830, it became the most widely read magazine in the United States and helped mold the taste and style of three generations of American women. It published stories by some of our greatest writers—and by others who are deservedly forgotten. The magazine's editor, a famous writer in her day, is remembered today only as the author of "Mary Had a Little Lamb."

2. This etching shows the first famous American actor. He was playing both comic and tragic roles on the New York stage while still a teenager. He was a black man, possibly born in Africa. Racism drove him from the United States in 1825, and he made his career in England, where he died in 1867.

3. Here is a piece of sheet music—"Beautiful Dreamer." In the days before recorded sound, Americans created their own musical entertainment at home, but this composer's songs were sung in concert halls, too. Born on the day Thomas Jefferson died, he wrote his first hit at the age of 20. He wrote dozens of popular songs, but he was a poor businessman and died in poverty in 1864.

4. I see you looking at that pistol—don't worry, it isn't loaded. It belonged to a woman whom the Sioux leader Sitting Bull used to call "Little Sure Shot." She perfected her marksmanship as a girl in Ohio, where she was born Phoebe Ann Moses in 1860. As a member of Buffalo Bill's Wild West Show, she amazed audiences with her shooting exhibitions with rifle and pistol.

5. This pair of handcuffs was used by the most famous stage magician of all time. An immigrant from Hungary, he was born Erich Weiss in 1874, but he became known by his stage name. He performed many sensational magic tricks, but was most celebrated for his escapes—from handcuffs, jail cells, shipping trunks, nailed packing crates, even sealed milk cans filled with water.

6. The motion-picture industry began in 1895. This studio photograph shows its first great "star." She made her movie debut in 1909, at the age of 16. By 1917, when she starred in *Poor Little Rich Girl*, she was known as "America's sweetheart" and was earning $10,000 a week. Later she became a founder of United Artists, one of the biggest film companies in Hollywood.

7. Be careful with this old record—it was made by the first great singer in the history of jazz. She was born in Tennessee, probably in 1894. After years of singing in small nightclubs in the South, she was discovered by a record producer who brought her to New York City. She won her fame as "Empress of the Blues" through the recordings she made between 1923–1933.

8. Push the start button on that VCR to see one of the first hit shows in the history of television—"I Love Lucy." Its star created the show in 1951, and later starred in two more series on TV. She was more than just a comedy actress though—she was a producer who helped develop entertainment television as we know it today. (You can decide for yourself whether that's good or bad.)

9. This guitar once belonged to royalty—"the king of rock and roll," as his fans called him. Born in Mississippi in 1935, he developed a singing style that combined the sounds of country music, gospel, and rhythm and blues. He became a star in 1956 with his recording of "Heartbreak Hotel." Over the next 21 years, he made hundreds of hit recordings and more than 30 movies.

10. Speaking of movies, that little model dinosaur was used in one by the most popular film director ever. He was born in Cincinnati in 1947, and was making films in Hollywood by the time he was 22. He's made several serious films, but it's his blockbuster hits such as *Jaws, E.T.,* and *Jurassic Park* that have made him a legend.

Can you identify these 10 figures of American popular culture? Write their names on the lines below.

1. _____   6. _____

2. _____   7. _____

3. _____   8. _____

4. _____   9. _____

5. _____   10. _____

Inventions that Shaped America

"We have catalogued the technology of this sector of Planet Earth," Sfazzz reported. "It was known 150,000 years ago as the United States of America. Like all cultures in this galaxy, its history was very much influenced by invention. We've identified a few inventions that were particularly important."

Glidjj studied the three-dimensional models on the computer. "Interesting," she commented. "Tell me, Sfazzz, what was this gadget called? And this?"

"Well, that's still a mystery," said Sfazzz. "We are pretty sure of how these inventions were used, but we don't know what they were called. Maybe the language program can help us."

1. "This heating device was invented by one of the culture's greatest figures, in the year they called 1744. It provided a more efficient way of heating a room than the planet ever had before, giving twice the heat while burning only one-fourth the fuel."

2. "This box with the handle was invented by someone called Eli Whitney in 1793. It was used to separate seeds from a plant fiber that they made into cloth. The invention made it practical to grow this plant widely in the southern region of the country. This led to the spread of a primitive custom called 'slavery,' and to a great war between the northern and southern states."

3. "This agricultural device was pulled by large four-legged animals. It was built by a man named Cyrus McCormick in 1831. It made it possible for farmers to harvest grain much faster than they could by hand. Farmers could grow larger grain crops. Because it took less labor to feed more people, the country's population could grow and prosper."

History Mysteries
© The Learning Works, Inc.

4. "This useful substance is elastic, it keeps out moisture, and it holds air. It was once produced naturally on Earth, from trees. In 1839, a man named Charles Goodyear invented a way to make it stronger and weatherproof. Automobiles were not invented on this planet for another 50 years or so, but their development would not have been possible without Goodyear's invention."

5. "This crude communications device could not even transmit voices—only clicks. It required wires to carry messages. And yet it made it possible for the first time for Earthlings to send information instantaneously over long distances. The first system was completed in 1844 by Samuel Morse. Interestingly, before then he had been better known as an artist than as an inventor."

6. "For many years, tall buildings were typical of American cities—'skyscrapers,' they were called. And this is the device that made them possible. It was invented by Elisha Otis around 1852. This species might not even have thought of constructing buildings of more than four or five stories without it. After all, they didn't discover antigravity for another 600 years."

7. "A table game and a large animal led to the development of this type of material. The game was called 'billiards,' and it used balls made from the tusks of elephants. A man named John Hyatt invented a substitute material for these balls in 1869. It was the first of a large class of materials that transformed industry and the way people lived. It took the place of wood, paper, plant fibers, animal skins, and metals in many products."

8. "This fencing material was vital to the Americans in developing their western region. They used it to keep large animals from wandering. Someone named Joseph Glidden introduced it in 1874. It made it possible for small farmers to homestead on the frontier—to the displeasure of ranchers, who had been making free use of public land to pasture *their* animals."

9. "The greatest inventor of this culture was someone named Thomas Edison. He used this foil-coated cylinder in the invention he called his favorite—apparently, the first sound-recording device the Earthlings ever made. Edison called it a 'talking machine.' The cylinders were later replaced by revolving disks, and the machine was given another name."

10. "A boy named Philo Farnsworth came up with the idea for this gadget in 1922. He was 16 years old—equivalent to a nestling of 480 on our planet. He called it the 'image dissector.' It could transmit a picture electronically by breaking it into a pattern of lines. This was a key to the development of a communications medium that seems to have brought down their civilization."

Can you identify these 10 transforming inventions? Write the names by which we know them on the lines below.

1. _____   6. _____

2. _____   7. _____

3. _____   8. _____

4. _____   9. _____

5. _____   10. _____

Sports Heroes by the Numbers

From the ex-slave boxing champion Tom Molineaux in 1810 to the multimillionaire stars of today, Americans have had their sports heroes—and the numbers by which we compare them. Bobby Bigfan, a wealthy sports enthusiast, is offering as an award a skybox at next year's Super Bowl football game to the first person who can identify these 10 American sports legends—*and* complete correctly the calculations suggested by their names and achievements.

1. In America's early years, horse racing was the most popular sport. The nation's oldest continually-run horse race is the Kentucky Derby. Start with the name of the jockey who won the first Derby, and the year in which it was run.

2. Baseball had become the "national pastime" by the time of the Civil War, and the first all-professional league began six years after it ended. The star pitcher of the National Association of Professional Baseball Players won 207 games in the short time the National Association was in operation, and later made a fortune in the sporting-goods business. Who was he? Divide your last answer by the number of seasons he pitched for the National Association.

3. American football developed from soccer, rugby, and town games played in colonial New England. The modern game, however, was developed largely by one man, a coach at Yale University beginning in 1888. He set the number of players on a side at 11, invented the system of downs and the quarterback position, and helped begin the custom of naming an annual "All-American" team. Subtract from your last answer the number of letters in his last name.

4. The greatest athlete in history may have been this man, a Sauk and Fox Indian born in 1887. He was a college and professional football star, a major-league baseball player, and a double Olympic gold-medal winner in track and field. Add to your last answer the year in which he won his medals.

5. The female equivalent of the last entry rose to fame in 1932, setting four world records in a single track meet and winning two Olympic gold medals. She also played tennis, baseball, and basketball, but her best sport may have been golf: In 1946 and 1947, she won 17 tournaments in a row. Divide your last answer by the number of U.S. Women's Open golf championships she won.

6. The 1936 Olympics in Berlin, Germany, made this athlete a legend. An African American, his performance embarrassed German dictator Adolf Hitler, whose racist theories maintained that Germans and other "Aryan" people were the supermen of the planet and would easily defeat America's "black auxiliaries." Add to your last answer the number of gold medals this athlete won.

7. This athlete crusaded for equal treatment of women in sports. She presented her case on the tennis court in 1973, defeating a former men's star in a celebrated "battle of the sexes" match. She dominated women's tennis for years, winning 20 Wimbledon titles in singles and doubles, and many U.S. singles and doubles titles as well. Divide your last answer by the number of U.S. Championship and U.S. Open titles she won.

8. Only one boxer was brash enough to call himself "the greatest," and he may have been right. He won an Olympic gold medal in 1960, and four years later was the heavyweight champion of the world. He became the only fighter ever to win the heavyweight title three different times. From your last answer, subtract the last two digits of the year he won the title for the last time.

9. This woman gave up a promising basketball career in 1986 to concentrate on track and field. Among her Olympic medals are two consecutive golds in the heptathlon— a two-day, multi-event competition—which she won in 1988 and again in 1992. Multiply your last answer by the number of events in the heptathlon.

10. One of the world's most famous basketball players was born in Brooklyn, New York, in 1963. He became the first player ever to play on NCAA, Olympic, and NBA championship teams, accomplishing the latter feat for the first time in 1991. Add to your last answer the total number of letters in his first and last names to find the winning number for the skybox.

Can you identify these sports heroes—and the correct numbers for the calculations? Write their names and the number you computed for each answer on the lines below.

1. _____   6. _____

2. _____   7. _____

3. _____   8. _____

4. _____   9. _____

5. _____   10. _____

Miscellaneous Mysteries

Trail of the First Americans

When I finally caught up with Pete Pothunter, I found a collection of Native American artifacts worthy of a museum. In fact, that's where they'd been stolen from—museums across the country. After the police led Pothunter off to jail, I catalogued what I had found. Pete hadn't bothered to label anything. He'd only wanted to have the stuff; he didn't care anything about where it came from.

1. There was a collection of stone tools. They had to have come from one of the earliest human cultures of the Americas. The first Americans are believed to have crossed a land bridge from Siberia to Alaska, now covered by the waters of the _____ . They used tools a lot like these.

2. Next were an assortment of long, thin, fluted spear points. They're called _____ points, after the New Mexico town near where they were first discovered. The culture that made them lived during the Ice Ages, about 10,000 years ago.

3. Here was a beautiful, scary wooden mask, carved from a living tree. The _____ people of New York still make masks like this. They represent figures from their ancient religion and were traditionally worn for prayers and ceremonies.

4. There were a lot of masks in Pete's "collection"—he could have started his own museum exhibit! I recognized one as a _____ of the Hopi people, carved from the root of a cottonwood tree. The word means "spirit" in Hopi and other Pueblo languages, but it also can mean a person who wears the mask during a ceremony and impersonates the spirit, or a small carved and painted figure used to remind children of their traditions.

5. I caught my breath. Here was a beautifully painted pot that must have come from Chaco Canyon, in New Mexico. It was one of the homes of the _____ , ancestors of today's Pueblo people. The name is a Navajo word meaning "ancient ones," or "they who have gone." No one knows why they abandoned their great stone "apartment houses" in the desert around 800 years ago.

6. And here was a shirt made of bison hide. I didn't recognize the tribe, but it surely came from the _____ culture. They lived by the bison, or buffalo, until the herds were exterminated in the 1880s. I admired the braided horsehair and elaborate beadwork that were typical of this culture.

7. Next I found a broad, flat stone. It didn't look like much—unless one knew it was a digging tool from "Snaketown," a community of the _____ people near present-day Phoenix, Arizona. (This is another name that means "vanished ones" in the language of the Pima people.) The canals they dug to irrigate their farms were used by pioneer settlers of a later day.

8. Here was another mask, made of cedarwood, from a northwest Pacific Coast culture. It was part of a costume worn in religious plays. Peoples of this culture would hold huge winter feasts, called _____ , at which they would entertain people from neighboring villages and present them with lavish gifts.

9. There was a small stone head which resembled the larger ones made in ancient Mexico. Figures like these were found among the _____ culture that flourished in eastern North America for 2,000 years. The name comes from the great hills of earth that they built, probably to honor their dead. Artifacts found in these hills speak of widespread trade of goods and ideas.

10. Almost forgotten in a corner was a wooden stick with a basket on the end. It was used in a game played by nearly all the Eastern Woodlands tribes. The game has been adapted as a modern team sport called _____ that is especially popular in Canada and the eastern United States.

I tagged all the items, packed them up carefully, and arranged for them all to be returned to the places they'd been stolen from—after they were used as evidence in Pete Pothunter's trial!

Can you fill in the blanks in the detective's report? Write the correct names and words on the lines below.

1. _____   6. _____

2. _____   7. _____

3. _____   8. _____

4. _____   9. _____

5. _____   10. _____

A Nation of Immigrants

The fax came from a lawyer in Los Angeles. "Our client, Mrs. Pauline Stern O'Brien-Taylor, died recently at the age of 105," it read. "In her will, she left $50,000 to 'my great-great-niece, or cousin, or whatever, Anne Kato Mendoza.' If you can prove that you're the Anne Kato Mendoza she was related to, the money is yours." That message sent me on a search for my tangled roots.

1. My great-grandfather, Raul Mendoza, was an immigrant from _____ . He came to California in 1914, fleeing poverty and revolution in his homeland. Of course, California had been part of his homeland until 1846, so in a way, he was coming home.

2. Raul married my great-grandmother, Barbara Yee. Her grandfather came to America in 1865 looking for work, and helped build the first transcontinental railroad. Like most Chinese immigrants before 1949, he came from the Toishan region. This is in southern China, near the great port city of _____ , in Guangdong Province.

3. My grandfather, Mori Kato, came from _____ as a child. His family had been farmers, and they worked hard and bought a vegetable farm in California. In 1942, their farm was taken from them, and they were sent to an internment camp in Utah. The United States was then at war with their native country. Too many people were worried about the "loyalty" of these people—even though my grandfather was in the U.S. Army, fighting in Europe.

4. My grandmother, Anna Velarde Kato, was born in the Philippine Islands. Her family came here in 1924 and worked as farm laborers. When they arrived, their ship landed at Angel Island, near the city of _____ . Between 1910 and 1940, it was the main immigration station for newcomers arriving on the Pacific Coast.

5. A far more famous immigration station was _____ , in New York Harbor. I went there looking for information about Pauline Stern O'Brien-Taylor. Between 1892 and 1943, more than 12 million new Americans passed through there. A five-year-old Pauline Stern had arrived there with her family in 1908.

6. Pauline's family were Jews from the city of Smolensk, in _____ . They came here fleeing religious persecution, and settled in New York City. About 2.5 million Eastern European Jews came here between 1880 and 1920.

7. Pauline married her first husband, an artist named John O'Brien, in 1922. His family had come from Ireland in 1849, fleeing the famine caused by the failure of the potato crop. Like many of the 1.5 million Irish who came here at that time, including the ancestors of President John F. Kennedy, they settled in _____ , Massachusetts.

8. Pauline was a widow for some years before she married Frederick Taylor in Miami, Florida. He had come there from Kingston, on the island of _____ , in 1964. About 1.5 million immigrants have come to the United States from the islands of the Caribbean since 1960, escaping poverty or repressive governments.

9. I found the connection! It seems that Pauline's grandson had been in the Marines during the war in _____ . He married a woman from Hue in 1975, one of about 400,000 refugees from that country who settled in the United States after the war. Now, it turns out that her sister—oh, never mind! Papers in hand, I was off to Los Angeles.

10. The lawyer was a man named Brahko Jeftic—an immigrant himself, from Sarajevo in war-torn _____ . "With a family tree like yours, you couldn't be anything but an American!" he laughed as he handed over the check. "It's still the 'promised land,' isn't it?"

Can you provide the missing place names in Anne's story? Write them on the lines below.

1. _____   6. _____

2. _____   7. _____

3. _____   8. _____

4. _____   9. _____

5. _____   10. _____

History Mysteries
© The Learning Works, Inc.

A Monumental Treasure Hunt

Good afternoon. You are about to embark on a nationwide treasure hunt. Each clue will lead you to an historic landmark or a monument to an event in American history. You'll have to visit each one to find the next clue, so don't waste time! Here is the first clue:

1. Begin at a statue of a soldier of the Revolutionary War. It stands on the spot where the first shots of America's War of Independence were fired and honors the volunteer soldiers who were prepared to fight "at a minute's notice."

2. You can see the next monument from far away, but you must travel there over water. A gift presented in friendship by France in 1884, it stands more than 300 feet tall and is recognized everywhere as a symbol of freedom and of welcome to new Americans. Look for the clue beside a poem, "The New Colossus," inscribed at its base.

3. Now go see a play at a restored theater. On the evening of April 14, 1865, the stagebill was a comedy—*Our American Cousin.* A distinguished guest was in the audience. It was not a very good play, and he attended only because his presence had been advertised. If he had stayed home, our history might have turned out differently.

4. In the Smithsonian Institution's National Museum of American History there is a huge American flag—only don't go there! Instead, go to the site where the flag once flew. It was there during a battle of the War of 1812 that Francis Scott Key saw this very flag flying "by the dawn's early light," and was inspired to write the words to "The Star-Spangled Banner."

5. Your next stop is not a national memorial, though it might have been if the South had won the Civil War. Just east of a state capital that once hosted the Olympic Games, you'll see some ghostly Confederate leaders on horseback sculpted on a rock wall.

6. It's time to leave the East Coast. Go to a school built by the hands of its first generation of students. The African-American educator Booker T. Washington founded it in 1881 as a school where black students could learn useful trades. Today it is a distinguished university and a national historical site. You'll find the clue in a museum devoted to the work of the scientist George Washington Carver, who worked here for many years.

7. Now visit the boyhood home of one of America's greatest writers. Beside the house is a white picket fence. It may have inspired the fence that "Tom Sawyer" never whitewashed. Nearby is the cave the writer knew of as a boy, in which Tom and Becky Thatcher get lost.

8. Head out across the Great Plains to a range of mountains shaped like a human heart. They are sacred to the Dakota (Sioux) people, who named them *paha sapa*, or Black Hills. Find the next clue at the visitors' center of a national memorial to four U.S. presidents, whose faces are carved into a granite cliff.

History Mysteries
© The Learning Works, Inc.

9. Next, go to a site named for a French-Canadian trader who built a cabin near here in 1820. Later, a log trading post and stockade were constructed here for exchanging goods with the Indians. It became a gathering place for Native Americans and mountain men and the first protected resting place encountered by settlers traveling westward along the Oregon Trail. In 1849, it was taken over by the United States Army.

10. Finally, go to the spot where the United States truly became united. It took the early settlers six months to cross the plains, mountains, and deserts to California. After the first transcontinental railroad was completed, it took only six days. You'll find the treasure at the site where the tracks from east and west were first joined by a golden spike, on May 10, 1869.

   Oh, the treasure? Sorry, it isn't anything golden. It's just the satisfaction of knowing all the things you do about our nation's history!

   Can you identify the sites of all the clues? Write their names and locations on the lines below.

1. _____   6. _____

2. _____   7. _____

3. _____   8. _____

4. _____   9. _____

5. _____   10. _____

Legends Tall and True

Separating history from fiction can sometimes be like solving a mystery. Did an event really happen—or has a story been retold so many times that it has become accepted as truth? Consider the 10 Americans whose exploits are described below. Some of the stories about them are true, while others "grew in the telling." See if you can name the colorful Americans they tell about.

1. His real name was John Chapman. He was born in Massachusetts in 1774, and he really did travel throughout the midwestern settlements planting apple trees as he went. At one time he owned about 1,200 acres of apple orchards. But he probably never wore a tin pot for a hat or a coffee sack for a shirt. These stories were first circulated long after his death in 1845.

2. She was indeed the daughter of an Indian chief whom the English settlers at Jamestown called King Powhatan. She may or may not have saved the life of Captain John Smith when she was 12 years old, but she and Smith were never sweethearts. She later married another English planter, John Rolfe, and traveled with him to England, where she died in 1617.

3. Now we come to a true "larger-than-life" figure—or rather, an untrue one. Stories of this giant lumberjack, his feats of strength and his great blue ox, Babe, circulated through logging camps of the upper Midwest about 100 years ago, but none of them are based in reality. In fact, they may have been created by a lumber company as an advertising stunt!

4. This man's story was based on a real event of the 1870s. He was an African-American laborer, working on a railroad in West Virginia, who accepted a challenge to dig a section of a tunnel faster than a machine could do it. According to the legend, he won and then collapsed and died of exhaustion. What is more likely is that he was crushed to death by rocks falling from the ceiling of the tunnel—after he did, in fact, win the race.

5. This frontiersman's reputation as a hunter and Indian fighter, "half horse, half alligator," was largely promoted in tall tales he told about himself. He was born in Tennessee in 1786. As an Army scout in 1813–1815, he did fight against the Creek Indians. Later, as a congressman, he opposed a bill to remove Indians from their lands. Tales about him grew after his death, which may or may not have occurred at the Battle of the Alamo in 1836.

6. This woman was born Martha Jane Cannary, but is better known by her nickname. She grew up in western mining camps, where she became an expert horsewoman and sharpshooter. She may have served as a scout for the U.S. Army, as she claimed, but she never rode with an outlaw band, as some movies have suggested. She became a true hero in 1878 for helping the victims of an epidemic in Deadwood, South Dakota, where she died in 1903.

7. A popular song of 1909 spread the legend of the bravery of this railroad engineer. On the night of April 30, 1900, his express was speeding southbound near Vaughan, Mississippi, when he saw that the track was blocked by two freight trains. Instead of abandoning the locomotive and saving his life, he stayed and jammed on the brakes. He was the only person killed in the wreck.

8. Let's go back to colonial days for a story of piracy on the high seas. In 1695, a New York trader and sea captain was commissioned by the King of England to capture pirates and French ships. Some time afterward, he may have turned pirate himself, or have been forced to do so by his crew. He was arrested in Boston and taken to England, where he was hanged for piracy in 1701. Many tales circulated about his alleged bloody deeds and his fabulous treasure, which some people believe still lies buried on or near Gardiner's Island, New York.

9. This woman was a seamstress in Philadelphia during the American Revolution, and she did make flags. But the tale that she sewed the first "stars and strips" at the request of George Washington was first aired by her grandson, nearly 100 years after the event.

10. Finally, we consider a symbol of the United States itself. He may have originated as one Samuel Wilson of Troy, New York, who supplied food to the army during the War of 1812. He would stamp barrels with the initials "U.S." Later, people connected these initials with Wilson's nickname, which by then had become an unfriendly nickname for the United States government.

Can you identify these 10 American legends? Write their names on the lines below.

1. _____   6. _____

2. _____   7. _____

3. _____   8. _____

4. _____   9. _____

5. _____   10. _____

That Good Old American Know-How

Americans have always been famous for their ingenuity in figuring things out and getting things done. To celebrate the progress of American science and technology, Rachel Rightway, a self-trained tinkerer and engineer, has left a working example of that ingenuity in a room of historic Willard's Hotel in Washington, D.C. Which room? That's for you to figure out, by identifying innovations and the people and places associated with them, and by doing the mathematical calculations suggested in these clues.

1. The first notable American scientist was also the first notable American statesman, publisher, and inventor. You've met him before in this book. Start with the year he performed his famous kite experiment, during which he proved that lightning was electricity.

2. The first automobiles were built in Europe, but it was an American working in Dearborn, Michigan, who first found a way to build them cheaply enough for average people to afford. His "Model T" was so inexpensive that farmers found it more economical to buy than a team of horses. Add the year in which it was introduced to your last answer.

3. This scientific instrument works by strengthening a beam of light. It can be used to cut through metal or perform delicate surgery, target a weapon or carry television signals, perform precise measurements or operate a compact-disc player. The first one was built by American scientist Theodore Maiman. Divide your last answer by the last two digits of the year it was invented.

4. The first American scientist to win a Nobel Prize for Physics was a designer of equipment that used beams of light to make precise measurements. His device made it possible to calculate the size of stars and measure the speed of the earth through space. Subtract from your last answer the last two digits of the year he died.

5. An American biologist was one of three scientists who discovered the structure of DNA, the molecule that carries genetic information. They found that it was shaped like a double helix, something like a spiral staircase. Multiply your last answer by the number of letters in the scientist's last name.

6. One of the most amazing feats of engineering was reversing the course of a river so that it flowed upstream. The river lies within one of America's largest cities, which has the same name as the river. The task was completed in 1900 to prevent sewage in the river from polluting Lake Michigan, the source of the city's drinking water. Add to your last answer the number of letters in its name.

7. In 1929, an American astronomer made the discovery that the universe is expanding, its galaxies moving farther apart. He died in 1953, and was honored years later by having the first orbiting space telescope named in his honor. Subtract from your last answer the last two digits of the year the telescope was launched.

8. Poliomyelitis, or polio for short, was once one of the world's most feared diseases. It left many of its victims permanently paralyzed, and outbreaks of the disease were common. Then an American scientist developed the first safe and effective vaccine against polio. Subtract from your last answer the last two digits of the year the vaccine was introduced.

9. Americans first landed on the moon in July, 1969. Everyone knows the name of Neil Armstrong, the first astronaut to step onto the moon. Divide your last answer by the number of letters in the last name of the *second* astronaut to walk on the lunar surface.

10. Personal computers are so widespread today, it's hard to believe that the first commercially available one was built only in 1975! It had 256 bytes of memory, and buyers had to put it together from a kit—and you'll find one in that hotel room, if you've done the math right. For your "lucky" answer, add to your last answer the number of letters in the computer's name, taken from the name of a planet in the TV series, "Star Trek."

Did you find the winning hotel room number? Write the answers and show your calculations on the lines below.

1. _____   6. _____

2. _____   7. _____

3. _____   8. _____

4. _____   9. _____

5. _____   10. _____

Answer Key

A Colonial Mystery
Pages 8–10

1. 1682
2. 1728
3. 1661
4. 1540
5. 1585
6. 1647
7. 1729
8. 1673
9. 1706
10. 1630

The Revolution Turned Upside Down
Pages 11–13

D   1765
H   December, 1773
A   April, 1775
J   July 4, 1776
C   September–October, 1776
F   December, 1776
E   September, 1777
B   December, 1777
G   August, 1780
I   September, 1781

Great-Great-Grandma's Civil War Diary
Pages 14–16

1. Fort Sumter
2. Manassas; Robert E. Lee
3. James Andrews
4. George B. McClellan
5. Emancipation Proclamation; Sharpsburg (or Antietam)
6. Stonewall Jackson; Chancellorsville
7. Gettysburg; Vicksburg
8. Ulysses S. Grant
9. William T. Sherman; Petersburg
10. Appomattox

Going West
Pages 17–19

1. Cumberland Gap
2. New Orleans, LA
3. Fort Mandan
4. Santa Fe, NM
5. Salt Lake City, UT
6. Sacramento, CA
7. Fort Laramie
8. Abilene, KS
9. Tombstone, AZ
10. Oklahoma City, OK

Into the 20th Century
Pages 20–22

1. Box camera (not invented until 1888)
2. Electric refrigerator (not available until 1930s)
3. World Series (not played until 1903)
4. Ice-cream cone (not invented until 1904)
5. Radio (broadcasting did not begin until 1920)
6. Father's Day (not established until 1910)
7. Olympic Games (not held in 1916)
8. Vitamins (word not used until 1912)
9. Flu epidemic (broke out in 1918)
10. Air fares (no commercial flights in 1920)

Answer Key

A Number of Heroes
Pages 23–25
1. 1947
2. 1931 (Thurgood Marshall: 1947 – 16)
3. 19,310 (Montgomery: 1931 x 10)
4. 742 (19,310 ÷ 26)
5. 751 (742 + 9)
6. 107 (Raleigh: 751 ÷ 7)
7. 428 (107 x 4)
8. 2405 (428 + 1977)
9. 481 (Selma: 2,405 ÷ 5)
10. 473 (Virginia: 481 – 8)

Vision of a Great Leader
Pages 27–29
1. Sacajawea
2. Sitting Bull
3. Hiawatha
4. Sarah Winnemucca
5. Pontiac
6. Osceola
7. Ely Parker
8. Susan Picotte
9. Joseph Brant
10. Sequoyah

O Pioneers!
Pages 30–32
1. Jean Baptiste Point du Sable
2. Daniel Boone
3. Elfego Baca
4. Jane Long
5. James Bowie
6. John Sutter
7. James Beckwourth
8. John Charles Fremont
9. William Sublette
10. Mary Jemison

Heroes in Peace and War
Pages 33–35
1. John Peter Zenger
2. Sibyl Ludington
3. Harriet Tubman
4. Robert Smalls
5. Susan B. Anthony
6. Chief Joseph
7. Jeannette Rankin
8. Alvin York
9. Dorie Miller
10. Cesar Chavez

In a Man's World
Pages 36–38
1. Elizabeth Blackwell
2. Elizabeth Pinckney
3. Sarah Grimké
4. Nellie Bly
5. Mary Lease
6. Amelia Earhart
7. Ida Bell Wells
8. Lillian Wald
9. Eleanor Roosevelt
10. Nellie Tayloe Ross

Answer Key

American Originals and Great Spirits
Pages 39–41
1. Benjamin Franklin
2. Sojourner Truth
3. Henry David Thoreau
4. Walt Whitman
5. P. T. Barnum
6. John Muir
7. Gertrude Stein
8. Helen Keller
9. Satchel Paige
10. Woody Guthrie

George Washington's Lost Diary
Pages 43–45
1. Lord Fairfax
2. Robert Dinwiddie
3. Fort Duquesne
4. Patrick Henry
5. John Adams
6. Morristown (NJ)
7. Daniel Shays
8. James Madison
9. New York
10. Alexander Hamilton

Clue 9: The site of Washington, D.C., was not chosen until 1791.

Searching for Abraham Lincoln
Pages 46–48
1. Larue County, KY
2. Spencer County, IN
3. New Orleans, LA
4. New Salem, IL
5. Springfield, IL
6. Lawrence, KS
7. Ottawa, IL
8. Chicago, IL
9. Gettysburg, PA
10. Richmond, VA

He Said *What?*
Pages 49–50
1. John F. Kennedy
2. Theodore Roosevelt
3. John Adams
4. Harry S. Truman
5. Calvin Coolidge
6. Thomas Jefferson
7. Franklin D. Roosevelt
8. Abraham Lincoln
9. Andrew Jackson
10. Richard M. Nixon

Answer Key

Literary Treasure Hunt
Pages 58–59
1. Mark Twain
2. Maya Angelou
3. Edgar Allan Poe
4. Laura Ingalls Wilder
5. Emily Dickinson
6. Carl Sandburg
7. Herman Melville
8. Dr. Seuss
9. Robert Frost
10. Louisa May Alcott

The Great Music and Dance Forum
Pages 60–62
1. Francis Hopkinson
2. Charles Ives
3. Isadora Duncan
4. George Gershwin
5. Duke Ellington
6. Maria Tallchief
7. Alvin Ailey
8. Leonard Bernstein
9. Jerome Robbins
10. Wynton Marsalis

Monuments to the Unknown
Pages 51–53
1. Millard Fillmore (1850–1853)
2. John Quincy Adams (1825–1829)
3. James K. Polk (1845–1849
4. William H. Taft (1909–1913)
5. Herbert Hoover (1929–1933)
6. Gerald Ford (1974–1977)
7. Benjamin Harrison (1889–1893)
8. Jimmy Carter (1977–1981)
9. Calvin Coolidge (1923–1929)
10. Rutherford B. Hayes (1877–1881)

Presidents by the Numbers
Pages 54–56
1. William Howard Taft; 1912
2. Zachary Taylor; 1862 (1912 – 50)
3. Woodrow Wilson; 133 (1862 ÷ 14)
4. James Monroe; 1945 (133 + 1812)
5. Grover Cleveland; 389 (1945 ÷ 5)
6. Dwight D. Eisenhower; 345 (389 – 44)
7. Ulysses S. Grant; 115 (345 ÷ 3)
8. Warren G. Harding; 460 (Ohio: 115 x 4)
9. Theodore Roosevelt; 466 (460 + 6)
10. Lyndon B. Johnson; 398 (466 – 68)

Answer Key

Painting of Mystery
Pages 63–65

1. Winslow Homer
2. Georgia O'Keeffe
3. Mary Cassatt
4. George Caleb Bingham
5. Frederic Remington
6. Frank Lloyd Wright
7. Benjamin West
8. Anna Mary Robertson ("Grandma") Moses
9. Jackson Pollock
10. Edward Hopper

Pop! Goes America
Pages 66–68

1. Sarah Josepha Hale
2. Ira Aldridge
3. Stephen Foster
4. Annie Oakley
5. Harry Houdini
6. Mary Pickford
7. Bessie Smith
8. Lucille Ball
9. Elvis Presley
10. Steven Spielberg

Inventions that Shaped America
Pages 69–71

1. Franklin stove
2. cotton gin
3. reaper
4. vulcanized rubber
5. telegraph
6. safety elevator
7. plastics (or celluloid)
8. barbed wire
9. phonograph
10. television

Sports Heroes by the Numbers
Pages 72–74

1. Oliver Lewis; 1875
2. Albert G. Spalding; 375 (1875 ÷ 5)
3. Walter Camp; 371 (375 – 4)
4. Jim Thorpe; 2283 (371 + 1912)
5. Mildred "Babe" Didrikson Zaharias; 761 (2283 ÷ 3)
6. Jesse Owens; 765 (761 + 4)
7. Billie Jean King; 85 (765 ÷ 9)
8. Muhammad Ali; 7 (85 – 78)
9. Jackie Joyner-Kersee; 49 (7 x 7)
10. Michael Jordan; 62 (49 + 13)

Trail of the First Americans
Pages 76–78

1. Bering Sea (or Bering Strait)
2. Folsom
3. Iroquois
4. kachina
5. Anasazi
6. Plains (or Plains Indian)
7. Hohokam
8. potlatches
9. Mound Builders
10. lacrosse

Answer Key

A Nation of Immigrants
Pages 79–81

1. Mexico
2. Guangzhou (or Canton)
3. Japan
4. San Francisco
5. Ellis Island
6. Russia
7. Boston
8. Jamaica
9. Vietnam
10. Bosnia and Herzegovina

A Monumental Treasure Hunt
Pages 82–84

1. Minute Man National Historical Park (Lexington, MA)
2. Statue of Liberty (New York, NY)
3. Ford's Theater (Washington, D.C.)
4. Fort McHenry (Baltimore, MD)
5. Stone Mountain (Stone Mountain, GA)
6. Tuskegee Institute (Tuskegee, AL)
7. Mark Twain Home and Museum (Hannibal, MO)
8. Mount Rushmore (near Rapid City, SD)
9. Fort Laramie (Fort Laramie, WY)
10. Golden Spike National Historic Site (Promontory Point, UT)

Legends Tall and True
Pages 85–87

1. Johnny Appleseed
2. Pocahontas
3. Paul Bunyan
4. John Henry
5. Davy Crockett
6. Calamity Jane
7. Casey Jones
8. Captain William Kidd
9. Betsy Ross
10. Uncle Sam

That Good Old American Know-How
Pages 88–90

1. Benjamin Franklin; 1752
2. Henry Ford; 3660 (1908 + 1752)
3. laser; 61 (3660 ÷ 60)
4. Albert Michelson; 30 (61 − 31)
5. James D. Watson; 180 (30 x 6)
6. Chicago; 187 (180 + 7)
7. Edwin Hubble; 97 (187 − 90)
8. Jonas Salk; 42 (97 − 55)
9. Edwin "Buzz" Aldrin; 7 (42 ÷ 6)
10. Altair; 13 (6 + 7)